HERE, HOLD MY WINE!

Robin's Practical and Impractical Guide to Life:
Vintage 2019

ROBIN F. ANDERSON

KWE
PUBLISHING, LLC

Anderson, Robin F.

Here, Hold My Wine! Robin's Practical and Impractical Guide to Life: Vintage 2019

Copyright 2019 by Robin F. Anderson

Cover Art by Ed Knight, Communications Art & Design, Inc.

Editing by McKayla Roberts

Publishing by KWE Publishing – www.kwepub.com

Any article written for any publication has been modified for contents of this book.

ISBN (paperback) – 978-1-7326273-6-9

ISBN (e-book) - 978-1-950306-00-8

Library of Congress Catalog Number: 2018967258

Printed in the United States of America

Robin F. Anderson

To schedule Robin for book signings and/or speaking engagements, please go to www.hereholdmy.wine or email her at robin@robinfanderson.com.

Acknowledgments

Credits to those who have helped me grow with my writing. They have encouraged me, taught me, sincerely had my best interest at heart, and have led me to success!

Shirley T. Burke – The first time I met Shirley T., as she is lovingly known to most, was when she was an aerobics teacher. She has always been a true inspiration, reading something to uplift us after class. She always has something positive to say. She happened to post a writing opportunity on Facebook. I was down and out for six weeks after surgery at the time, and sent an idea to the CEO of an online magazine, and that is how I received my start with writing. Thank you, Shirley T., for the suggestion to start writing an article for the first time!

Brenda Krueger Huffman – Brenda took a chance on a very inexperienced writer and groomed me to bloom into an inspirational writer for her online magazine, *Women's Voices Magazine*. When Brenda chose me as one of her top 20 columnists for my work to be syndicated all over the world, I asked Brenda what was the criteria for her selection of me. I will never forget Brenda's words. I. My articles were always on time, 2. All my work was original, 3. The number of 'hits' I received from readers, and 4. She stated her husband thought I was hilarious. Thank you, Brenda, for the countless hours of editing for not only me, but all of your writers. Your encouragement has propelled me to the next journey in my writing endeavors.

Dennis J. Pitocco – Bizcatalyst 360 – Publisher/ Editor-In-Chief - Dennis has been fantastic to work with and posts my written stories all over the world. My business articles are published in the Execubrief section, which reaches 'C' level executives in many countries. Dennis has invited me to participate in helping non-profits through *Goodworks 360* as well, of which I am a participant. Thank you, Dennis, for supporting me with your fantastic edits and quick commu-nications. It is a pure joy writing for your publication.

Dr. Mike Jernigan PhD – Averett University – Mike was the teacher that came into our room on the 1st night of going back to school as an adult, and said something that was totally untrue. I spoke up and said I felt what he was saying did not make sense, and he stated that typically, when someone knows you are a PhD, they will never question what they say. He stated that night was a test of our partic-ular group. And, our group continued with our BBA steps in an accelerated program. Mike pushed all of us to continue to go after our MBA, which we did. Mike has always been a cheerleader for my career advancements and my writing. It is always nice to have such a supportive teacher and mentor. Thank you, Dr. Jernigan, for your continued support and encouragement!

Kimberley W. Eley (Kim) – KWE Publishing, LLC – Kim has been extremely helpful to keeping me focused and excited about my book. Kim has been understanding of my hectic work life, and has been extremely supportive of my hopes and my dreams. She knows how to take an idea that I have and make it sound better than I was ever thinking it could be. She is a fantastic editor and has helped me learn a lot about how this book should be laid out, which stories needing expansion, and helped me understand what intrigues readers to read my work. Best of all, she actually laughs at my jokes and really likes my wine!

A lot of working sessions did include my inspiration. Wine! Never an enthusiast of wine in the past, but I have become one over the years. I enjoy learning everything about the wine industry and the ever-present struggle for that gold and double gold honor. Thank you, Kim, for the wine you have brought to our working sessions, and the wine and food we have consumed at my home going over painful details that really needed to be done. I could not have done this without your help and support. Now...we need to celebrate with a nice dinner and several bottles of great wine! Cheers!

Publisher's Note

As soon as I met Robin, I just knew we were going to have a great adventure! Collaborating with this amazing lady is such a joy. She radiates positivity! I'm delighted whenever we meet that no matter what life challenges are happening at the time, she always has a big smile and can find a way to laugh about it.

Writing a book is a journey. There are highs and lows, to be sure. I know whenever we work together (and I can hardly call it work), we will have a great deal of fun, we will laugh a lot, and I will feel a million times better than I did before! And we might take a quick writing break to sneak off to a winery...just saying!

Thank you for making our collaboration into a real friendship. Cheers to you, Robin!

Kim Eley, KWE Publishing LLC

About the Author

Author **Robin F. Anderson** has been described as a self-made success, a phenomenal manager whose work with Fortune 500 companies has made her a hot commodity. But it wasn't always that way.

Robin earned her Clerical Certificate right out of high school at Rappahannock Community College. Years later, while raising her son alone after a difficult divorce, she went to Averett University and earned her BBA and MBA in an accelerated program all while earning a 3.88 GPA. She was inducted into the Pinnacle Honor Society for the volunteer work she did during her university years.

Robin went on to work for a number of Fortune 500 companies: Reynolds Metals, First USA, Paymentech, J.P. Morgan Chase, and American Express (AMEX). Recruited by AMEX, Robin was hired as Director of Implementation, where she ran a very successful team known internally as 'The A Team.' After 7 ½ years at AMEX, Robin was hired by SunTrust bank as a Vice President, Commercial Card Officer. Robin was recruited this year by a smaller bank named Texas Capital Bank to help with another Commercial Card start-up. She is now a Senior Vice President, Commercial Card Implementation Consultant.

Over the years, as she surpassed the expectations set for her, peers have speculated that Robin was born with success, or that everything has come easily for her. Robin shares her down-to-earth, practical methods through which she earned her success in her personal and professional life.

Contents

Introduction - Merlot, Is It Me You're Looking For?

OK, so you picked up this book and you're wondering if it's any good. Well, I can tell you this much; if you ever find anyone who has been through as many things as I have and are still left standing, then you know I'm someone who can't be stopped.

Yes, I am a force to be reckoned with and I did not get this way because it was easy. I have had many people come to me and ask me how I became so successful in life. Well, I believe, it's 'the thought process' that got me to where I am today. To me, a challenge is only a challenge. I will find a way around that hurdle no matter what and keep moving forward. Nothing stops me from achieving my dreams.

So now you are thinking, "this is going to be one of those boring 'self-help' books that everyone writes?!" Well, you are wrong, my friend. And here is the reason why. I have always been able to move forward. Nothing cripples me. Certain things slow me down a bit, and I, like everyone else, have a tendency to self-doubt every now and then, but darn it-these 'things,' as I will call them, only make me stand up on my own two feet and fight harder.

However, there is only one 'thing' that seems to get to

me, and I am very confused about it and struggle with it. Maybe, just maybe, you can write back to me with some suggestions. Let's see how good you are at figuring out what that 'thing' is while you are reading my epic stories.

And speaking of stories...when you read my original stories, or should we call them, 'real life drama,' the 'things' that happen to me are almost unbelievable experiences anyone could have, and with such bad luck. Bad luck...is there such a 'thing'? You know what they say about karma. I guess I have really pissed off someone along the way.

So, should I tell you early on the crazy things that happen to me? Nah...I want you to read the book, so there you have it. Now you at least know I'm honest. But I gotta tell you, the best people around have told me I really don't have bad luck, bad stuff (aka 'things') happens to everyone. Wow, are they optimistic, and they really don't know me yet.

I am sure by some people's standards, I have had it easy. Other people have said, and I've heard, "I have no idea how you do it." Honestly, I do not know the difference in experiences because I can only judge based on what I had to go through in life and what I needed to survive.

I hear all the time, "Well, you have a fantastic job and live in a big home- seems to me you have not ever had a hard life!" People tend to judge me based on where my life is now rather than take the time to realize that most people, including me, have had a long journey to get where we are ending up. And where you end up is really in your own control.

I have been through a lot in life. Some good things have happened and many bad things have reared their ugly heads in my life. But, I have always taken the 'bull-by-the-horns,' so to speak, and changed the direction in my life by having a certain 'thought' process.

So by sharing my stories of life's ups and downs, I will

hopefully give you a guide to my overall thought process, how I tackled each and every obstacle, and the decisions I made to keep moving forward in the direction I wanted. Hopefully, you can apply the way I approached challenges to make your life better.

As a single mother, it's not been easy. I remember when one day when my son was about three years old, he decided to take my red fingernail polish and 'paint' the wall. Do you know how hard it is to cover red fingernail polish on a white wall? How is THAT repair going to happen? You want to know a secret? But, you can't tell anyone, OK? I would meet a new guy and find out what he did for a living and put him in my 'little black book.' When I needed repairs done, I knew who to call. A simple cooked dinner and voilà...repair done! Come on, I know you have been ingenious to do the same before, right? Now that I am older, I do have to pay for my repairs. When did THAT actually happen, anyway?

But, I chose not to make being a single mother an excuse for anything that happened to me. Life is choice, although it was not my choice to be a single mother. But, how you choose to live life is your choice. So things happen. There is not a person around who does not have bad things happen.

Many people do the 'why me' every day. My stories are about ways you can look at things differently, and make your life exactly what you want it to be!

Well, you are still with me, so that is a good sign. Maybe my luck is about to change. It's nice to have you along for the journey. And what an incredible journey you will read in the chapters. Let's get started...Hold on to your glass of wine or beer because it's going to be funny, sad, and sometimes you might even get a good idea or two along the way. Oh, and see if you can find my creative 'wineisms,' aka wisdoms, along the way!

Now turn the page and let's get this party started!

Section 1 - Early Childhood and Growing Up - Rhone Wasn't Built in a Day

OK, HANG IN THERE WITH ME...YOU GOTTA KNOW MY ROOTS BEFORE YOU CAN UNDERSTAND ME!

Chapter 1: Working For the Nuns

Manischewitz wine was the choice of our church priest!

～

I GREW UP IN A VERY SMALL TOWN BETWEEN RICHMOND AND Williamsburg, Virginia. I was raised in a good Catholic family and attended grade school at our church where the entire class had to wear navy and white uniforms. I really did not think much about it back then, but nuns all looked the same in their habit uniforms and the students (both boys and girls) looked the same in their matching outfits and crew socks. It was a very simple time back in that school because you did not argue with your parents about what you would wear to school each day. Shame it can't be that way today, right?

The classroom was not really that large, but we had two grades in each room. The teacher would give one grade a lesson and then would shift to the next grade on the other side. I remember being in first grade, learning my numbers and how to read for the first time, and when I finished first grade the following year, I was able to sit on the other side. Because of that, I think for the first time in my life I started to take pride in my accomplishments.

Grade school brings me to my first funny story. OK, this is a good one!

I will never forget one day when I was in second grade when one of the students decided she did not like what the nun wanted her to do. I heard the nun and the little girl arguing about something and the next thing I knew, the little girl picked up one of the small wooden chairs in the room and cracked it over the nun's head. The entire class immediately picked up their heads from the reading assignment. The nun yelled at us to keep our heads down and not look up again!

Back in those days, we believed if we did not listen or obey, we would really be in trouble and would be punished because it would be a sin. In fact, in those days it was not uncommon for someone to get whacked across the knuckles with a wooden ruler. So, maybe you can understand why we listened! We obeyed the nun and any adult who gave us an order.

That little girl went far beyond what we were taught to do and would do anything we were not told to do. She certainly was a rebel, and I think about her all the time and wonder whatever happened to her. I was way too chicken to ever do what she did... but, as you will find out, I got my own stride on later!

Go ahead and laugh, but one thing I kept wondering was, "Do the nuns have hair?" Back then, the nuns were fully covered and had those hard kind of white cones around their heads, so the only thing sticking out were their face and their ears. I would try to look in their earhole to see if they had hair. OK, I'm just being honest here! I do have strange things about me. Don't judge me. It was sort of funny because on the overweight nuns that white thing around their face would squeeze their cheeks and made them look rather funny. The skinny nuns looked okay, so I guess they only had a 'one size fits all' back then. But I did finally figure out they really did have hair!

Those were the years I finally learned responsibility. The nuns told everyone in the school- grades 1 through 5- they were offering fifty cents a day to sweep the floors after school. Back in that time, believe it or not, I was very quiet and shy. (Yeah, I did not think you would believe me.) I took that job because nobody else wanted it and I felt I was helping in some way. I remember I had to use this orange, wet kind of rubber-smelling stuff and then I would sweep the floor. It was pretty neat because it would stop the dust and move the dirt pretty good so I could put it in a dust pan and throw the dirt in the trash.

Helping is something we learned as kids. I guess that was the start of me paving the way to stepping up when I could. And to this day, I really do feel I learned my respect for others in that very small Catholic school. I was not taught to hate or see people differently. And I still feel the same way today. I continue to preach that if we all have respect for each other, regardless of ethnic background and beliefs, our world would not be in the turmoil it is in today.

Before I knew it, my elementary school days at my Catholic school came to an end. Now, I had to go to a public school. And what an adjustment that was to my Catholic upbringing.

ERE, HOLD MY WINE MOMENT:
Giving back is something we all should continue to do. Look to help those less fortunate. If it means you do not buy something expensive but help someone in need instead, it will make you feel so good inside. You can take pride in yourself helping people who really need help.

Chapter 2: Public School - Life is a Chardonnay, Old Friend!

Wow, we both graduated in the book to the 6th grade. I think we just may be friends by now!

～

THE SCHOOL DID NOT HAVE THE FUNDING TO CONTINUE OUR Catholic school, so I had to attend the rest of my school years in public school. My first day of public school is a day I will never forget. Kids seemed out of control and I heard language I had never heard before.

When I was called on to answer a question in my science class, I stood up next to my desk to answer the question as I had been taught all my life. I was quickly reprimanded by the teacher, "Robin, that is fine and dandy to do in your Catholic school, but do not do that in this school." I will never forget her words.

I went home crying that day and I thought my life was over. I did not understand how I would function in that school because the behavior was so foreign to me. I had to learn to adjust to survive. Eventually, in high school, I did manage to adjust and make the new school life work. One of my best moments was one day in English class. We had to pick a poem and work with someone in the class to figure out a way to bring out the meaning of the poem. My partner and I decided on an Edna St. Vincent Millay poem about a wife who was notified her soldier husband had been killed in action.

My partner's only part was to come to the door and announce I had lost my husband during the war. From there, I was supposed to sit down and read the poem. When we went to present, my partner aimed the spotlights on me in a way that was so bright I had to struggle to read the poem. I read each word really slowly, so it looked like I was putting feeling into the reading when actually, I had to strain to see the words.

When I finished, the teacher stood up and said, "Bravo, the best reading I have ever heard. Have you ever read poetry before?" Of course I told her 'no,' but was thankful I did not blow the assignment! How I managed that day, I still have no idea, but we got an 'A' on our effort!

Learning to be 'good on my feet' has been profound to my success in life.

Soon, I branched out and wanted to do other things in school. I went out for the cheering squad and actually made the team! I think my many years as a dancer really helped as I had taken ballet, tap, and baton for many years since the age of five. When I went off to college, I branched out to learn jazz and modern dance. Dance certainly became a passion of mine. However, my dream of being a Denny Terrio and a *Solid Gold* dancer would not be my future, but it was a dream nonetheless!

OK, if you are asking who Denny Terrio and the *Solid Gold* Dancers are, then you are a little younger than I am, but suggest you look them up because they were awesome!! The TV show *Solid Gold* was a big hit! OK, so maybe you had to be there, but trust me, it was every little girl's dream to be a dancer on that show.

*H*ERE, HOLD MY WINE MOMENT:
When your life dramatically changes, don't give up. Learn to adjust and move forward. Sometimes in life, you have to be a chameleon, moving quickly to shift and blend in when you need to. You don't have to be liked by everyone else, but you can hold on to your beliefs and still find a way to co-exist.

Chapter 3: September - Back To School - "Ice Wine, Baby"

You can sing along with me on this one! Do you remember the days went by so fast and suddenly you had to return to school? But, I always loved school, so I was OK with it....hang in there with me....let's go back to school together since you are now my best friend!

SEPTEMBER ALWAYS MAKES ME THINK BACK TO MY SCHOOL days. I was always excited to get back to school and see my friends. I was a B minus kind of girl, but going to school has always been enjoyable to me.

I went to a very small high school where I graduated with forty-six people. The memories and relationships have stayed strong over the years and I know no matter what happens in life, I can always go back home to that small town where there was a lot of love and friendships made over my most informative learning experiences.

I learned so much from the early years but I am not talking about books. I am talking about learning how to deal with all kinds of relationships. We all experienced bullying in some form or fashion and we all probably bullied someone and did not realize the hurt we were inflicting at the time.

I am of Polish decent. And yes, I was made fun of. I am sure some of you even know those jokes. But, it was okay, because I know who I am and very proud of my parents and my grandparents.

All of my family was very hard working and did their best in life like everyone else. The personal struggle and sacrifice my great grandparents had to save their children was so hard to believe. If I asked my grandparents about their parents, they would just cry thinking about those times.

You see, back long ago, the Polish people were being killed in the same concentration camps that you hear about with the Jewish people. So, in order to save their children, they would put their small children on boats to foreign lands to save their lives. I cannot even imagine how hard that would have been to let your small babies go to a foreign country knowing you would never see them again.

Now I brought a tear to your eye, but the struggle was very real back in those days. You have to truly understand the sacrifice and the sincere love they had to have for their children in order to let them go and hope for the best.

The small town I lived in was one of the best places to grow up, but I too was bullied. I was made fun of because I had a 'ski' type of nose. And yes, it was an ancestral nose. I actually fell one time and broke my nose. My parents made me stop my bike as cars went by on the road, but my cousin behind me did not realize I was going to stop and caused me to fall on the road and break my nose.

The most embarrassing thing ever was going home and my father taping up my nose. Back then, you did not run to the doctor for everything, so my father actually set my nose himself. I had to go to school the next day with a round 'Rudolph' looking nose, except it was white tape rather than being red. Talk about kids laughing and making fun of me! Ugh, that hurt so much, and not just from the pain of the break.

I needed compassion, empathy and understanding, but instead I was ridiculed. Who could blame the kids hurting my feelings? I probably would have done the same thing at that young age.

But everyone was made fun of at one time or the other. It hurt my feelings, but I was OK because I knew the kids would not be hateful to me forever. I was just the 'butt' of the joke that day, or should I say, the 'nose' of the joke? Is there such a thing? Well, it was for me!

I remember one time in my early days of Catholic school, a good friend of mine had a very extreme case of poison ivy. She was outside crying and I asked my teacher if I could go outside and be with her.

The nun allowed me to sit with her, but the only thing I had to offer was being with her as she cried from the pain of her sores. I learned what compassion, empathy, and under-standing could do to make someone's pain bearable by simply offering for them not to be alone. In some small way, I hope she never forgot that day and how I really wanted to help her. I just cried with her. And, believe it or not, she and I recently found each other again on social media and it's like we never skipped a beat. We are still fantastic friends today and we lean on each other, hearing each other out with the trials and tribulations we have both had in our lives. There is comfort there to be able to reconnect with someone who I grew up with and still love and trust so fully today.

I also connected with another girl with whom I grew up in my public-school days. We were friends and cheerleaders together. She too is a fantastic woman, and I am amazed how we've been able to connect again and share experiences. We can be there for each other. Never discount your early day friends and try to reconnect with them. The rewards are fantastic!

The hard knocks and lessons from all of my formative years has built who I have become today. As a matter of fact, people have commented that I am too nice. (Really?) I really do not understand how you can be too nice but I guess I still have some work to do. However, I strongly believe you can be loving and caring and still set boundaries so you are not taken advantage of, which, yes, has happened to me too.

You learn every day in life. The learning will continue until I am gone from this earth, and then who knows what is in front of me 'up there'?

But we have to be careful when others hurt us. We can all go into a negative direction and take the bullying and hurt to heart, becoming bitter. In some cases today, kids stop dealing with the hurt and pain in a horrible way that devastates families.

So I challenge you to think back to your innocent days, days in which you may have been hurt and needed help.

Did someone come to your aid?

Did you help someone and did not realize the impact you made on their life?

Everyone you touch in life is there for a reason. I do wonder why some were brought into my life to make me unhappy, but I realize it is also a lesson to me as well.

And believe me, when I get 'up there' one day, I will have a heart-to-heart talk with The 'Man' and ask a lot of questions!

So your school supplies you need are:

- Compassion

- Empathy
- And Love for people in your life and those you have yet to meet.

*H*ERE, HOLD MY WINE MOMENT:
Remember, you have control over how you react to things. I could have chosen to be the victim. Instead, I chose to laugh at myself. I know some people who would want people to feel they were hurt worse so people would feel sorry for them. Take the high ground if you really are not hurt but just have a bruised ego. Everyone has silly moments in life. Just laugh about it and move on. People like people who are happy better than being grumpy!

Chapter 4: Fifty Shades of Nuh Uh!!!!

Don't open the wine before it's time!

~

I WAS IN HIGH SCHOOL, AND MY PARENTS HAD STRICT RULES about dating. At fifteen and a half, I could double date. It was not until I was sixteen that I was actually allowed to go on a date alone. So, I accepted a date with a guy I had actually met when my mother and I were shopping.

My mother immediately took to the very personable guy, so he asked for my phone number and I gave it to him. In a few days, he asked if I wanted to go out with him, so I said yes. I was very excited to actually go on a date with someone who was acceptable to my mother.

The guy picked me up on a Saturday evening. I could tell the guy was a little nervous because he kept asking if the temperature was OK or if I wanted to listen to something different on the radio. Then he started driving down a side road and I asked where we were going.

He pulled into a road not very well traveled in the woods; he stopped the car and told me to put out or get out.

I asked if he was serious and he said yes, so I got out of the car, ran back to the side road and ran as fast as I could to get away from him. I could hear him backing out and knew I had to hide, so I jumped into a spot in the woods. He rode past and could not find me.

As he drove back and forth, I hid until I could get back home. That night, I walked all the way home. I came home early, but luckily my parents were in bed. Mom spoke up from the bedroom and asked how my night was, and I told her it was fun.

When Mom asked about the date the next day, I just said we rode around a bit and came home early. I told her there was not much going on in town and we decided to call the night early. I told her he was nice, but not really my type. I never wanted my parents to know what happened since I handled the situation by myself.

One thing I have always demanded is respect. If someone does not respect me, then I stop the interaction all together. It was a very frightening night for me, but one I was able to handle. I was lucky. I am hoping that guy really did think about what he did, hope he learned a lesson that night, and never did that again.

I never saw him again and I was very glad about not seeing him.

Over the years, there have been some men who have made advances in the workplace when they were married or with someone else. I never understood why men would approach me this way, but I was always able to control the situation. Maybe I was lucky, but I made sure I did not give into anything they were offering. And I am very glad I did not.

Later, as you will find out, my own situation was very hard on me. If I am worth anything to the guy, he will do the right thing and end the other relationship before I will consider even going out on a date. Of course, there have been some who would not tell me they were with someone else, but luckily these days it is very easy to find information. Even back before the computer, people talked and eventually, you found out who you were dealing with and that their intentions were not true.

I believe you need to respect yourself at all times. I have seen some people who really do not respect each other and it is a very sad thing to see happen. I have coached some women on 'men' issues and some men on 'women' issues. It seems it's always easier to help others, but yourself, not so much!

I have been very selective about who I date. It's a shame, but some people think I am gay just because I do not date someone steadily. I even had a co-worker one time come up to me before a meeting and in his best Northern accent say, "Hey Anderson. You are a good-looking woman. I never see you with a guy. Are you gay or something?" I laughed and told him that I am not gay, just very selective.

I do not feel I need someone in my life just because people believe you should be coupled up or they think there is something wrong with you. I believe we all need to make ourselves happy. I am happy with my wonderful friends, my work, and generally the life I lead. I just keep moving forward and know one day, I will meet my prince charming. As time moves on, I do want to concentrate more on finding Mr. Right, but as the name suggests, I will meet him when the time is right.

$\mathcal{H}$ERE, HOLD MY WINE MOMENT:
You do not have to fit a mold in society that you have to be a certain way or live a certain way. The right people will come into your life. Just be patient.

Chapter 5: Community College

Onward my friend...we are on an education roll now! This sounds like a good 'sparkling' wine moment. Always celebrate accomplishments and continue with your education – always!

BEFORE I KNEW IT, IT WAS TIME FOR COLLEGE. HIGHER education typically brings you new friends. It's a time when some of your older friends are not active in your life, so it leads you to build new relationships.

I'm glad you are still my friend from the start of this book and you are now going to college with me. Funny stories ahead, so hang on to your wine!

I enjoyed continuing my dancing. I wanted to continue, but did not want anyone to know I was a dancer because I did not want to teach classes. I just wanted to take the fun dancing classes. My first day in dance class, the teacher told us to get down on the floor and 'stretch out.' The teacher immediately saw my stretch and said, 'you have dance experience, come up here.' Darn it!! I was exposed.

She immediately reached down and grabbed my ankle and stretched out my leg to the side and said, "This is the turn out you are trying to achieve," as I grimaced in pain. Ouch!! Never do that to someone who is not stretched out yet.

A turn out is how your leg looks when you put your leg to the side with toe pointed...it's hard to explain, so just go with the flow here. There will not be a quiz after you read this, so you are safe!

So, guess what I had to do for the rest of that class year? Yep, you guessed it: help teach. But I did learn new jazz and modern dances. So, that part was fun anyway.

However, my goal in school now was to learn more about business. My parents did not have a lot of money, but they agreed to pay the tuition of the community college of $75.00 every quarter if I paid for the books. I took a job as a part-time secretary for the administrator of the college to help pay for my books. I quickly figured out he really enjoyed having someone at his every whim.

The dean of the community college system was very picky, and knew what the spacing should be on typed letters, etc. I was working very hard one day on a letter that was going to the dean. Suddenly, the intercom sounded off with my boss asking me to come "see him in his office." I immediately went to his side. He asked me to get him a cup of coffee.

Now he had asked for coffee numerous times. However, the coffee urn was located at my desk. He made me walk all the way to his office for him to ask me for coffee. I had to walk all the way back to my desk to get the coffee, and then walk back to his office to deliver it to him.

I have to tell you, this was the first time I stuck up for myself. I do not know what got into me, but this time I said to him as I walked around to look under his desk, "Are your legs broken? You know I have to get that letter out in a few minutes. Can you not get up and get your own coffee, or at least tell me what you need on the intercom so I can save some time?"

He apologized, and he did stop asking me to get his coffee. However, I knew I needed to get out of that small town if I was going to make a name for myself.

*H*ERE, HOLD MY WINE MOMENT:
Go with your instincts. When you need to move on, do it without fear. Just get an idea or a goal in your head and just go for it! After all, people can certainly get their own coffee, right?

Section 2 - Career and Other Adventures

TIME TO CATCH A 'CAB' OF LIFE AND MOVE
FORWARD...TIME TO GROW REALLY GOOD
GRAPES AND MAKE SOME GREAT WINE!

Chapter 6: Began Career

OK, now we have our first real job – you know, not the Dairy Treat kind of job but a corporate type of job! And yes, I'm glad you are still with me. More embarrassing and funny stories ahead. Caution: Time to refill your glass.
Wine tasting is typically of the newest wines and not always wine at its best taste if a red. Drink the white now and let the red 'cook.' I call it cook anyway! Cook – aging in 'normal' terms.

I CONTACTED A PLACEMENT AGENCY AND TOLD THEM I WANTED a job in Richmond. I took the battery of aptitude tests, and they came up with a position as a bookkeeper at Davenport & Company, a stockbrokerage firm.

The girl I was replacing was going on maternity leave. She taught me how payments came in for the purchase of stock. I learned the correct procedures and entries quickly. I will never forget a very embarrassing moment when she saw me using my fingernails to take staples out of the documents. She asked if I knew what a staple remover was, and needless to say, I did not. I was straight out of business college that had showed me all kinds of business writing and math, but nothing of practical experience. So, I was the 'butt' of the joke that day.

Probably one of the funniest days came when I was helping out with opening the mail. New carpet had been installed the night before. Back then, you had a plastic thing you rolled your chair around on, but you did not have those fancy wheels on your chair like you do now that will roll on carpet.

I remember preparing to hand over the mail to the person who was sitting directly behind me when I pushed off my desk as hard as I could to roll back and hand her the mail. When my wheels hit the carpet, I completely flipped over and landed wedged between her desk and the turned-over chair. (OK, as I am writing this memory, I am sitting here laughing as hard as I can right now...) At first, I was not sure if I was hurt or not, but I remember being extremely embarrassed and that I could not physically move.

The person whose desk I was wedged into was trying not to laugh, and she did come around to help me escape the attack chair. Plus, our boss, who had a wall of glass surrounding his office, saw the whole thing and ran out as well, trying to conceal his laughter. It was pretty funny. I was laughing, but tears were also coming down my eyes because once I started moving, all I could feel was pain. They were able to push me to the side, so I could escape the chair tightly locking me in a most awkward position. Lucky for me, I was wearing pants that day. Whew!!

Yeah, you don't think that was embarrassing, do you? I was humiliated. Right after that, we had our annual Christmas party and the whole place was laughing at me. At that point, what could one do but laugh with them?

I did find it interesting that every day when the stock

market would close at 4 pm, they had an open bar free to all of the employees. It was rather nice having any drink you wanted while you worked the last hour of your job, but then the drive home was interesting.

The bad part was since this was my first venture away from home, my parents would drive over an hour each day and wait in front of my apartment to make sure I got home okay. Really? Yep, they sure did. But, when I think back on it, they only did it out of love, but thankfully over time, that stopped. It was hard for them to let go. I understand.

You know, we all could react differently and get angry or mad at someone making fun of us, but I really think it takes the stronger or better person to just look at the weird and strange things that happen to us and just see them as life's little lessons. Heck, I don't know about you, but at this point in my life, I'm going to stick around just to see what else happens. And yes, just sometimes find the humor in 'things.' It will certainly make your life a lot happier.

$\mathcal{H}$ERE, HOLD MY WINE MOMENT:
Do not be afraid to do something different or something you are unsure about. Failure is something that is going to happen, no matter who you are. Learn to laugh at yourself. Keep respecting people, and keep standing up for yourself.

SPECIAL HAPPY HOUR MOMENT

THE ROOMMATE

When I moved to Richmond for my first real job, expenses were very tight and I really needed to get a roommate. A girl I worked with at Davenport & Company told me about her girlfriend who was also looking to find a place. Perhaps, she said, we could share an apartment.

I met the girl and she seemed very nice. It seemed the arrangement was going to work out nicely because she worked at night and I worked during the day. She moved in my apartment into the other bedroom. As time went on, she brought her dog to live with us, which was fine by me. I always loved animals and he was a beautiful golden retriever.

One day, I came home from work and apparently the dog had a major diarrhea problem that day. She was cleaning it up and said she was getting someone to clean the carpet. Again, those things happen and I was fine with her taking care of the issue.

Then things started changing. She apparently got a

boyfriend. When she came in at midnight when she got off from work, they would fix food (that I paid for) and never cleaned the kitchen. They were very loud with the TV going and would smoke pot. Now I am not a prude, but when I was trying to sleep, that smell would make me sick to my stomach.

Every morning, I would have to get up and clean the messy kitchen. They never did dishes and I never had any food left! And, I had a tendency to go back to my parent's home on the weekend. I had most of my friends there, so before I made a lot of new friends, I would go back home where I felt comfortable.

One time I came back to my apartment and it was like a moment out of a fairytale book. Someone had been sleeping in my bed. Literally!! I knew my roommate had a girlfriend who would visit, but apparently she took it upon herself to not only sleep in my bed while I was gone, but also go into my closet, wear my clothes, and find a bottle of liquor I had bought so I could have friends over and have something to drink. My bottle was almost empty.

I had never had anyone that felt it was okay to help themselves to someone else's private property. Needless to say, I had to ask her to move. I realized that some people were not raised like me and felt they could do anything they wanted with my food, clothes, and property. Everything was 'fair game' to my roommate.

Another time, I had a friend whose husband ended up cheating on her. She had nowhere to go, so thinking I knew her, I had her move in with me. Quickly I found out that she had a revolving door of men coming to 'visit' her. It was not a good situation with my son at home, so eventually, I had to do what I could to get her moved into her own place.

We did manage to stay friends, believe it or not. Then,

she moved in with a very nice guy, who I thought was really good for her. Then she admitted that she was sleeping with his friend and apparently many other guys. I never lived this kind of life, so it was hard for me to understand this type of behavior. She had lived a very different life than I had, so I tried to understand.

One night, her boyfriend called me and he had suspicions. He asked me what I knew, and I gave him a tip. I know it was wrong to betray my friend, but I hated how he was being treated. I just told him maybe the next time he went out on a business trip, he should sit outside of his house and follow her to figure out the truth.

Needless to say, he figured out what was going on. She called me and was furious with me. I saw them once after that. He came over to talk to me and she immediately grabbed him away from me and forbade him to talk to me ever again.

I never saw them again and a friendship was destroyed. But it made me realize I did not want to be associated with something or someone who went against my beliefs. Gee, now I sound like a prude, but how would you have handled it?

Since that time, if I ever had someone move in with me it was only to help someone, not because I needed a roommate. Let's just say, most of the time, I prefer to live by myself until that ultimate guy comes into my life anyway!

$\mathcal{H}$ERE, HOLD MY WINE MOMENT:

Remember, you will have to deal with things you never thought you would encounter. Take a sensible approach to handling the conflict if you can. It's better not to create enemies if you can in life. You never know when they will pop back up in your life!! But, remember to learn from the experience and move forward, never making that mistake again hopefully. After a while, you do learn people pretty well and can make better selections in the future. You really want to be surrounded by people who are true friends.

Chapter 7: Working For Reynolds...And The Turtle!

OK, so now I was moving up to the 'big leagues' of companies. You ready to take this venture with me? Well, at this point, you and I are tight friends, so you have no choice!!

~

AFTER WORKING FOR THE STOCKBROKERAGE FIRM, THE placement agency did their job and managed to get me an interview with the company of my dreams. My brother worked at Reynolds Metals Company (which is now a part of ALCOA). I was very nervous but excited to interview with them for a position in their Accounts Payable Department as an accounting clerk.

Back at that time, Reynolds Metals, along with Phillip Morris, was a top notch company in the Richmond, Virginia area. I wanted to work at Reynolds since my brother was there, as it gave me some sense of comfort. Reynolds was one of the largest companies in Richmond at the time, and it was very hard to get into the company unless you had contacts. While my brother worked there, honestly I never disclosed he was related to me. I wanted to get this job on my own merit, and I did!!

I was also newly engaged to be married, too! Juggling everything- I needed to plan a wedding and learn a new job- was a big challenge, but I think it was the first time I knew I just had to dig in and get it all done. I set my mind to just getting everything done, learning my new job, and just not thinking about how hard it all was to do!

Planning a wedding and starting a new job was not easy, but it was a very happy time in my life. I think this is the first time when I really learned to multi-task. I had to learn how the Accounting Department paid bills, so it was learning a whole new way of doing things. I was very proud I could bring my new knowledge to the job...remember, I now knew how to use a staple remover. OK, so you laugh now, but it was big, OK?

It was challenging to learn everything a big company does, but then after work, I was picking out a wedding dress, figuring out what my bridesmaids were going to wear, choosing the food, and deciding everything I needed for a large wedding. And, to make things more stressful, my mother even invited the mayor of our small town because.....now get this one, she went out on a date with him once. Not twice, but once, and I did not even know this man.

Oh well...it was my mom, so I had to do it.

My specific role at work was matching purchase orders with invoices and receiving reports to ensure payment to suppliers. I quickly learned my tasks, and I wanted to learn more about the department.

One of the people in the department was going out for vacation. Rather than let that person's duties just sit while she was gone, I offered to cover her tasks while she was absent. My boss agreed to my request and I was excited to help the coworker so when she came back, she could feel like she really did have a vacation. Honestly, I have worked at many jobs where if you took time off, it really was not worth it because so much work was either backed up or done incorrectly by people trying to fill in for you.

I worked hard to keep up with both jobs that week. I asked if I could do the same when others took vacation. Soon, I had learned just about every job in the department! My boss certainly liked it, but I think my coworkers were a bit jealous. They certainly did not have the ambition I did, but they could have done the same thing. They chose not to do anything but their own job, day in and day out.

My boss thanked me for what I had done and was smiling all the time when he gave me new tasks and I handled them all. My coworkers, of course, would roll their eyes and not talk to me, but that was all right because I knew I just had to do this for me. Learning new jobs kept me from being bored with my job.

I have heard so many people complain about being bored with work and how they hated to go into work to do the same thing each day. Try doing what I did by learning each role in your department. Talk to your boss. He or she will be excited that you are eager to learn and you will become a more valuable employee.

I also reached out to other departments to understand what happened before and after my duties. Understanding the entire workflow really helps to piece everything together. You become more understanding of the end-to-end process, not just what you do each day.

Actually, my boss saw how curious I was and soon gave me a new opportunity!

I was in the same department, but now worked in the travel area. This department was responsible for paying all of the expense reports for the company travelers.

I always loved learning about our sales team, and could live vicariously through their expense reports from places I had never been before. One day, my boss came to me and said we had a lunch meeting at a local seafood restaurant with our travel agency partner. I was thrilled to actually be a part of my first business meeting.

Dressed in my best business suit and trying to have great table manners, we ordered drinks. After two drinks I was a little tipsy, but needed to go to the restroom. I only hoped I could walk straight without embarrassing myself. Because we were at a seafood restaurant, I was surprised when I got to the restroom entrance and had two choices before me, Inboard or Outboard.

Now I don't know about you guys, but even sober, I would have stopped on that decision. I did not have the luxury of the little man and woman on the door, so I hesi-tated trying to quickly think what decision to make.

Luckily, a man came out of the Outboard door and my decision was quickly made. He just looked at me and smiled. I know he had to see the fear on my face as I was pondering my decision. My first business meeting went off without a hitch and I loved being included in such an important meeting.

It was not long when the travel part of our department grew and I had a new boss. He was very different from my first boss as the new man seemed very strict and we worked very quietly.

We quickly nicknamed the new boss "Turtle" because he was very bald and when he laughed, he looked...well, like a turtle. I will never forget his office- a corner office in the building with one big plant that climbed all the way around the office.

One day the Turtle, who wore cufflinks, was watering his prized plant. His cufflink snagged the plant and the plant started to come down off the walls. He was fighting the plant as if he were being attacked. Since I was the only person to see this happen, I was laughing quietly so hard that I looked like I was crying.

The other workers could not figure out what had me so tickled. The Turtle even came out to ask me a question. I had to pretend like I was looking for something in my desk so I did not get in trouble for laughing. He soon left my desk thinking I did not see him.

I finally composed myself long enough to start to quietly tell my coworkers what had happened, when at the same time, the Turtle came out of the office with dead leaves off of the plant to throw in the trash can. Needless to say, I was dying laughing again. It's a pure wonder I did not get caught. Many years later, I did tell the Turtle what I had seen and he laughed and said, "Yes, that darn thing had me and I did not know if I was going to break free." One thing I never confessed to, however, was calling him "The Turtle"!

One day, the Turtle had a big scratch on his bald head. We took turns going in to ask him any kind of questions so each of us could assess the scratch on his head. It was pretty funny what we did to entertain ourselves at his expense. Yes, we were like mischievous school kids, but it made our workday very interesting too!

It goes to show you the boss is just like us, but with more power. Most leaders know it is okay to laugh, so talk to them about things that happen and they will respect you for striking up a conversation. I have become a boss who really does try to keep an open mind and just laughs at the things that happen. Laughing certainly relieves stress in the workplace and life in general.

Our office had been moved to the very large controller's department. Our new senior manager would walk through several times a day and we quickly learned to tip each other off when the boss was coming.

The code word 'butter' became our chant to warn the group to keep heads down and work while he made his daily, multiple trips. Although this man seemed to be stern, he had something he felt he needed to change, and actually, used me as an example one day.

I had a traveler who came to see me about not receiving his reimbursement as quickly as he had wanted and this man was very upset. Even at a young age, I learned that people typically have something going on in their lives that makes them so angry and upset in their demeanor. You know the type, they sort of have that 'bitch-faced look'? Yeah, I thought you knew.

I had this man in my cubical and had just started talking to him. I found out he had some personal issues that were causing him pain. All I could do was to listen to him. Actually, listening was all he really needed to calm down. I promised he would get his check in a few days, and he left thanking me and smiling.

My boss had gathered a group to listen to how I handled the upset traveler. Later he came up to me and stated how he admired me and felt I was really good with people. The biggest compliment he gave me is when he stated his New Year's resolution was to be 'more like me.' Wow!! Isn't that the coolest thing ever?

Respecting people includes listening and understanding what is important to them. Never forget that how others perceive you creates your brand, and is the best thing you can do for you and your career.

When my immediate supervisor decided to retire, I thought I may have an opportunity to move into a management role. I expressed my interest in the position. I worked diligently to do both my job and the supervisor's duties while the position was open. In the end, I did not get the job because I did not have my actual 'degree.' That only gave me incentive later to get my degree one day when my son was old enough to understand that momma was going to school at night.

ℋ ERE, HOLD MY WINE MOMENT:

One of the greatest traits a good leader can have is to learn empathy. Throughout my upbringing, I have always been keen on getting to know people. Understanding what is going on, knowing when they are not at their best, and helping them through tough times has helped me to be a respected leader. If you truly care about people you work with, they will respect you for caring and will always remember how you made them feel.

Chapter 8: Marriage and Challenges - A GoodMeritage Can Last for Many Years, or Can Be Gone in an Instant

Boy, now the dog poop gets much deeper! Let's see, what wine goes with poop...oh heck, just grab what you like and read on! This is a tough one to handle, so it might be a 'shot' kind of night.

⌇

I DECIDED IT WOULD BE A GOOD TIME TO START OUR FAMILY since my husband and I had been married for several years. I asked my husband his thoughts and he agreed. I wanted to make the decision together because it was important to me to raise our child together, not alone.

Within a few months, I was expecting our first child. I was about three months pregnant when my husband and I went to his company's Christmas party. I noticed a girl my husband worked with was looking at him. I mentioned my observation and he felt I was just acting jealous. I took his word that I was 'seeing something that was not there.'

My baby shower was being planned by some good friends and my husband wanted me to invite the girl I had seen at the Christmas party. So, I put her name on the list and she did come to the event.

When our son was born, my husband did not go into the delivery room with me and my doctor was furious with him. While in the hospital, other fathers would come by in the morning, at lunch, and after work. My husband would only show up for ten minutes before visiting hours were over at night. I was so upset because I did not understand why he did not want to be with us. Finally the day came to take our child home. My doctor explained to my husband that I had a very bad cold and he wanted me to stay in bed and not take care of the baby until I was well.

However, when we arrived at home, my husband got us in the door and explained he was going to a friend's house to play cards. Dishes were piled up and laundry was over-flowing. I managed to get our son settled in his room and I proceeded to do laundry and dishes. I was a new mother and just could not understand why my husband did not want to be at home with us. Finally, at two am, I called his friend's house and asked to speak to my husband.

But he just asked how the baby was. I asked when he was coming home, but again was just asked if the baby was all right. I said the baby was okay, but I was sick, very scared, and wished he would come home. He stated to me, "I will be there when I get there."

I hoped things would get better, but my husband would hardly hold the baby. Instead, he was staying out all hours of the night. I remember working seven days a week for a few weeks to catch up on a project. I had to come home every few hours to take care of the baby because he would not feed him or change him if needed.

One day my husband said he was going to move in with his sister because he could not get used to having a 'wife and kid.' I believed he just needed a break. I believed at that time that he just needed some time and would be back, so I helped him pack up a few of his things, and off he went. He agreed to give me $50.00 every week for the baby's care. At the time, I was attending a local community college to learn computer skills.

Unfortunately, my continued education had to come to an end because I could not afford a baby sitter. I had to stop school. The $50.00 each week only went for a daytime sitter and I could not afford to continue with my education since I was going to night school. The $50.00 did not help me with any other expenses and I had no food for myself.

Times were hard both financially and mentally for me. My son was only six months old and his father had left us. I can remember counting pennies and putting them in wrappers so I could get gas to make it to work. It took everything I had to afford food and diapers for my son. I had no food and it was very difficult for me. I felt very alone.

And I know most people would say I should have gone on some kind of assistance, food stamps or other help I could possibly get from the state, but I was determined I was going to make it on my own.

After a few months, my husband had sent papers to me to sign. The papers were separation papers. I realized then he was not coming back to us and I was devastated.

Through all of the turmoil, I never missed work, and not a single person knew my husband left. I was embarrassed that my marriage was over. I had never felt so lost in my whole life.

My next-door neighbor said I was wasting away. Little did she know I did not have any food.

One night my neighbor said, "You and I are going out and Alan (her husband) is going to stay with your baby." I had never been to a bar before, but we went out for a drink. Suddenly two guys walked into the bar and my neighbor said, "Hey, what about those two cute guys?" I looked up reluctantly and realized I knew one of the guys. Soon, he came around and asked me if I was Robin Anderson and I said yes.

It was the husband of the girl from the Christmas party. He stated while I was pregnant, he had caught them together and almost killed my husband. I simply asked, "Why didn't you?" This guy told me he wanted to tell me, but was afraid I would lose the baby. Guess I should have listened to my instincts.

I called my husband the next day at his work and asked him to meet me at the house during lunch. By the time my husband met me, the news had reached him about what I heard. I asked him if it was true and he said it was. My heart broke in a million pieces. I asked why he did not tell me and he stated, "You were the best wife and mother and I did not want to hurt you."

At some point, what can you do? I simply looked at him and said, "I always heard a stiff dick had no conscious." We both laughed for a moment, but it did not change the fact that he was in love with someone else.

I would go to my parent's house, which was an hour away, on weekends to eat and take home doggie bags of food. I never told my parents, but somehow they knew how desperate I had become, or at least my mother knew what my situation may be like.

One weekend while sitting on the front step of my parents' house, my husband and his girlfriend rode by in a Jeep. He had talked me into getting a personal loan for this Jeep while he had a clear title and I was still paying for when I did not even have money for food. They waved and tears streamed down my face.

Months later, I was on the floor playing with my son and suddenly, I just lost it. I was crying uncontrollably. My son took his first steps and put his arms around me and hugged me. I knew at that moment that I had to do this for him, for us.

I had to pull myself together, and I decided to set goals. I vowed I would one day get back into school. For pleasure, I decided to start planning my dream house. Maybe it was an unrealistic goal to plan a dream home, but I needed something to focus on, something to strive for one day.

When my immediate situation stopped me from continuing my community college computer classes, I noticed my boss and his boss were treating me differently. I worried my job was in jeopardy even though I had not missed one day of work because of my husband leaving.

I finally went into my boss' office and told him what I had observed and asked if my performance had dropped. He told me he and his boss did not like the fact that I had quit school. He stated he believed going to school showed ambition.

I had to stand up for myself. I closed the door to his office and I told him I did not want to tell anyone at work, but my husband had left and I had to quit school because I could not afford anyone to take care of my son while I went to school.

Now, here is where I 'broke bad,' so to speak. I then stood up from the chair, and with finger pointed at him, which my mother told me never to do, I told him that ambi-tion to me was going to a community college right out of high school, and working to put myself through school. I told him his parents handed him his four-year degree from Princeton on a silver platter.

As I started to leave his office, I stated I would go back to school once my son was old enough to understand me going to school and when I finally earned my degree, I would hand him my degree on my own silver platter.

I turned around and headed back to my desk. I sat down and realized that I probably managed to get myself fired. My heart was beating out of my chest. What had I done?

It did not take very long when he came in my office and shut the door behind him. He sat down in a chair and apologized to me. He stated he did not realize what I had been going through. He offered his support and said he knew I would go to school when I was able to go back.

It was not long after my conversation with him that his boss called me in his office and told me confidentially he was creating a new concept of a department. Three manager positions were opening up and he wanted me to take the one he felt was the most challenging role. A senior manager had 100% confidence in me to be able to stretch myself to be the Supervisor of Technical Support!

I learned that sometimes, you need to take risk in order to branch out of your comfort zone. Now I am not advocating anyone rush out and tell their boss off like I did, but instead to understand when the right time is to defend yourself. Never be afraid to take on something new.

As a boss today, I look for a type of person with a spark in their eye. Make sure your management sees your ambition and willingness to pay your dues and work hard. Branch out, do different things, step up, and do more. Go to work early and stay late sometimes- rewards will come!

In my new role as the Technical Support Supervisor, I was able to tap into what I did best and that is being creative. I was able to automate various payments for our Accounts Payable group with new technology. My ideas were finally able to be unleashed. I finally made my mark with senior management.

*H*ERE, HOLD MY WINE MOMENT:
I believe if something is worth fighting for, then fight. Be respectful. Make sure the facts are on your side, and always, always, do your very best so someone does not have any reason other than to help you get to the next level in life and career.

SPECIAL HAPPY HOUR MOMENT

PARENTING MOMENT

My school days remind me of a lot of great things and how my strict rearing helped me be the person I am today. Things are so different now, and I often wonder how lives would be changed if those values were still taught and in place today. My tactics as a mother were probably unusual at times. Here is a quick little story.

My son was probably six years old at the time. He would walk from my place to my friend's house and 'pick up' her son to walk to the school bus together. She would watch them out of the window until the bus came to pick up all the children. The kids would be mortified if a mother was out there back then.

One day, my son apparently woke up on the wrong side of the bed, so to speak, and he was grumpy. I gave him breakfast and sent him out the door to start his short walk while I watched him to his destination where my girlfriend was waiting with her son. Now, you might want to picture this, but fair warning, it wasn't pretty.

I was not ready for work yet and had taken a shower,

wrapped my hair up and was in my robe. I stood outside watching my son in my horrible outfit each morning, but hey... a mother has to do what she has to do, right? Well, this particular morning, my grumpy son threw down his book bag outside and said he wasn't going to school. Of course, I told him he was going and to pick up his bag and go now or he would miss the bus. He continued to say he wasn't going, so I ran after him and he quickly picked up his bag and headed in the right direction.

So, you can imagine this picture now. Me with my hot pink robe (obviously a Christmas gift I did not pick out) and a yellow towel wrapped around my hair, chasing my son down the sidewalk until he got where he needed to go. HaHa!! Sometimes, you gotta do what you gotta do, right? Parenting isn't always pretty.

Chapter 9: Things Will Not Change
Unless YOU Make a Change...

Did you know? There was a wine called Engel Milk Wine. It was an agricultural wine other than a standard wine. It was produced and bottled by Casa De San José in Palmer, Alaska. It was 11% alcohol by volume (great day!!) and was made with powdered skim milk yeast and refined cane sugar. (From The Joys of Wine, Harry N Abrams, Inc.)

SO MANY THINGS ARE HAPPENING IN OUR WORLD TODAY AND some people feel there is nothing they can do to improve their business or personal circumstances. Jobs are stressful at times and family issues are always at the forefront of our minds.

So how in the world can people change and shift the way their life is going? Is it even possible? You bet there is a way!!

Since you have read to this point in the book, you know my personal life has not always been comfortable. There was a time in my life when I w e n t hungry to make sure my infant son had food. I've washed clothes without laundry detergent because I did not have money.

However, I am not complaining because the whole experience made me pick myself up, dust myself off, and move forward.

When my ex-husband had my son on a visitation weekend, I started cleaning a home to make ends meet. It gave me the money I needed to secure my son's care as I worked my regular job. I knew I also needed to do something at work that would help me move up the ladder and make a better salary.

I had to decide what I was going to do at work that would show my ambition to learn and my willingness to do more. I had a job I did not like and wanted to do something different. I was not going to get away from that position unless I did the best job I could.

I had people at work that disliked me, treated me poorly, and unjustly labeled me at times. These types of issues are nothing new to most of us, and there are a lot of people who have these problems and more. But there is a way to make a change.

How in the world do you change something when you have no control? Well, you do have power. Whether it is personal or work issues, make a plan to improve the problem. Get advice from someone you trust to help coach you with ideas of how to make a change.

For example, if you are in a job that seems to be stagnant with no upward momentum, you may feel you are stuck and have no way to do anything to get out of that role. However, one of the changes I did was to become more visible.

It was not long doing this volunteer work that other managers in other departments started noticing when they needed something and the person they usually talked to was not there, I could help them. When we had a vacancy in the department, I was the go-to person to help fill in for the position until the new hire was on board. I gladly did the job and trained the new person too! In some cases, I earned the position as my full-time job. And even though it was not a promotion, I gladly made the change to keep my mind fresh with learning new things. No matter what happens in life, keep a smile on your face, have positive attitude, and people will gravitate to you.

Have you ever spent time around the 'grump' of the department and wonder how this person can be so unhappy with life? Sure, I felt down at times and wondered how I could go on, but I never showed that side to coworkers or my boss. People always felt they could come to me with questions or an issue, and I would help them solve the problem. Nobody wants to be around a grumpy person.

You know the grumpy person. The one you avoid at all costs, even now? Well, I have a way to help solve that issue too. Strike up a conversation. Ask them to go to lunch with you.

Typically, that person just feels isolated. They think nobody likes them (which pretty much they caused themselves but will never realize it).

I have a friend who has a strong Southern accent. She calls the 'not so pleasant' people 'grumpy butts.' Can you just hear that name calling in your head with a strong Southern accent? It's funny, but I find those people fascinating, and will do whatever I can to make them smile in spite of themselves.

Eventually, I was running the department. You see, things will not change unless you make a change. You have to want a change bad enough to make things happen. And, if things do not happen right away, make more changes and keep going. It will work!

One time, I was in charge of giving a change management class. I was trying to figure out a smart way to grab people's attention. After all, we have all been in a classroom whereby we were about to fall asleep, right? So, after I spoke for about an hour, I could see the crowd with 'glazed looks' of, 'I would rather be anywhere but here.' So I told the participants we were breaking and to come back in ten minutes. When they came back, I had changed all of the name cards to a different seat.

They grumbled for a good fifteen minutes moving their things and complaining they wanted to sit by their friend, or by the door, or whatever the excuse was at the moment. They finally realized what I was doing, and all started laughing, and from that moment, we went off the actual book and had an open discussion about change. We all had a blast after that and everyone participated and enjoyed the class.

Personally, I also try to do what I can to give back. I've been fortunate to do well in business. I have a ton of friends whom I adore and on whom I can call anytime I need them. I love meeting new people who become life-long friends as well. Of course, there are those people we meet that we may never see again, but everyone we meet is someone significant in our lives.

My way of giving back is sometimes my writing, and another way is impromptu encounters. One day I was at Costco, and I decided to look at all of the cashiers and find the one with the 'grumpy' look. I got in that lane, and when it came time for this person to wait on me, I smiled and said, "I heard you are the best cashier in this place, so I wanted you to check me out." I surprised this person, and after that, we were laughing and high fiving each other. People around us both thought we were crazy, but it was OK. We were having fun and, for a moment, I made a difference in a life.

Some people just need to know they are good enough. They need to feel appreciated and cared for. Bosses need to recognize people more rather than putting fear in people just to feel they are in control by being so strict.

A happy workforce will always do more.

Recently, I happened to be in a place where I saw a young girl in her late teens crying. I looked her way and said, "Are you okay?" She said, "yes" as she was wiping her tears and came over to me. She told me her family had been having some issues and she just did not know how to deal with it.

I talked to her for a few minutes and assured her all would eventually be alright. She hugged me and thanked me for being there for her. At that moment, she felt a little better, a little stronger, just knowing someone she did not even know cared. And you know what? The comforting I did only cost me time. We are all rushing so much in this lifetime that a few minutes to help someone in need, even if you do not see them again, is worth the effort you put in to help them.

And, if you have not figured out by now, my reaching out to people is my way to change not only me, but the world around me. Maybe you should try it too!

ℋ ERE, HOLD MY WINE MOMENT:

If you knock on the door and it does not open, knock on it louder in a different way. Be the catalyst to the change you seek.

Chapter 10: No Money But I Had a Goal...House!

Create the good wine, my friend, and they will come!

As I mentioned earlier, I had to have something to wish upon other than a star. I started planning to create and build my dream home. I did it with no money in hand, but had fun cutting out pictures of what I liked. I took a pencil in hand and etched out my dream.

When married, the garage was all about him. The garage was why we bought the house. The house was not much, but we managed to make it a home. This time, I was building this dream in a way that was all mine. A fantasy perhaps, but a goal nonetheless.

My start to my design was a Better Homes and Gardens magazine house. I made changes to the layout, but I liked the expansive outside decks.

When I did the design, I went to an architect to do official blueprints when I was finally able to afford them. You have to start with a blueprint before anyone can give you a price to build the home.

I remember when I decided on the builder and had a meeting with the architect and the builder. They asked me things like, "Do you really need that dual-sided fireplace in your bedroom?" And I said, "Yes I do. How else do you think I am going to 'get a guy' without one? Take out the kitchen cabinets. I will buy those later." Needless to say, they shut up at that point and I got my cool fireplace. SCORE!!

It took twelve years to get to the point where I could finally afford to build my home. It took pushing myself up the ladder, getting new jobs, and taking on more at work, but once I finally got to a comfortable salary, I built my home and moved my mother in with me. She actually designed her own suite within my home. Actually, it is a whole separate house that is attached to mine!

*H*ERE, HOLD MY WINE MOMENT: Don't let anyone stop your dream. Only you can control your destiny. Make a plan and be patient. I waited a very long time to realize my dream, but it happened. Never give up!

Chapter 11: Can A Broken Heart Experience A Funny Side? Yep!

A kiss from a Rosé!

I AM SURE MOST OF US HAVE HAD OUR HEARTS BROKEN AT some point in our lives. I thought about a time in my life when I went through a pretty hard time. I will explain how it all went down, and how I handled the breakup. But most importantly, I will tell you how I picked myself up one night I was hurting. To this day, this is the first time I have ever told anyone the whole story about what I did that night.

I remember about a year after my divorce, I wondered if I would ever meet anyone that would help heal my heart. When you are trying to start your life over, but have an infant at home, restarting a life can be a challenge. But one day I did meet a guy who turned my world around in an instant. We spent a lot of fun times together in the short time we dated. He had his own small children and my having a little one did not bother him at all. He was that dream guy for me, the kind of guy and connection I never thought I would have again in my life.

During the time he and I dated, I was living in a new townhouse. My next-door neighbor said she could hear us laughing through the walls. He and I really did have that much fun together. We seemed like the perfect couple, or at least I thought we were the perfect match.

We dated for a few months. Then one Friday, he called and asked if I could meet him at a dance place across the river. He suggested I bring a friend who could meet his friend for a double date. So, I asked my next-door friend to go with me and luckily, she agreed. She and I traveled across to the other side of town and within a few minutes of our arrival, the guys walked in as well. We all sat down at a table and I could tell my guy was not his usual happy self. I asked him if something was wrong, and he said he would tell me later so it would not ruin our night.

How are you supposed to wait until the end of the night when you know something is wrong? I asked him to just tell me what was going on. He told me that the night before, his old girlfriend stopped by to talk and she spent the night. Needless to say, my heart broke in an instant. Never in a million years did I think he would have those words come out of his mouth and those words would stab me in the heart. He told me he did not know what to do and he was very confused. So, I just told him he owed it to himself to find out if she was what he wanted. I felt if he stayed with me, he would always wonder if he made a mistake. He immediately told me he never expected me to react with such understanding, and hugged me. As I melted in his arms, I held back the tears of the inevitable good-bye I never anticipated.

When I left that night, I was in a lot of pain. And my neighbor had a bit too much to drink and was not feeling her best. We were both a mess as I drove us home. Luckily the police did not pull us over that night. Can you imagine what the officer would have seen? Me, crying my eyes out with my makeup running down my face and her slurring her words and doing everything she could to keep from getting sick in the car. We both just wanted to get home. We finally arrived home and as soon as she got out of the car, she threw up in her front yard. I felt so bad for her and she felt horrible for me too. I made sure she got in her house, then went next door to my home and cried all night long. The next morning, she called to check on me. I wasn't any better and she was still sick. Needless to say, that day she and I didn't move from our homes.

Weeks went by and she and I decided we needed to get out of the house, so we went to a local spot. While there, one of his friends came up to me and told me he was asked to relay a message that my former guy stated he spent the day with this other girl and didn't know what he was thinking. This guy stated he asked that I hang in there. Unfortunately, that message gave me hope. But I did not hear from him, which only kept me brokenhearted.

The next weekend was Halloween, and all of my friends wanted me to come out and go dancing with them. Everyone was dressing up to go out for the haunted evening, but I was just too brokenhearted to think of going out. I did not want any of my friends to see how sad I was, so I told them I was staying home. After a few hours went by, I decided to stop feeling sorry for myself and dressed up to go out. After my son was fast asleep, I call my babysitter in the neighborhood to come over so I could go out for a few hours. I did not want anyone to know who I was, so I went out as a character I planned a few weeks before that was in a commercial years ago. I was going to be a 'California Raisin.'

For those of you who do not remember the California Raisin commercials, a 'bunch' of raisins danced around in white sunglasses with white gloves and black boots to the song, "I Heard It Through the Grapevine." They were promoting, of all things, California Raisins. Those commercials used to be pretty popular. The costume was fantastic to hide from everyone. I had purchased purple material and made a round garment to mimic a purple pumpkin and stuffed it. I used some of the material to hide all of my hair (as people would know me back then by my blonde hair) and then I had brown tights on to cover my arms and my legs. I put on white sunglasses, black mini-boots, and white gloves. I hope you at least have a vision in your mind of this outfit. Certainly not a sexy anything in this outfit! But, I was ready to 'wow' the crowd incognito!

I walk in the door and was immediately amongst the witches, werewolves, and sexy bunnies. I was the only California Raisin. I certainly had people looking at me and people stated I had a pretty cool costume, but I had to change my voice. Nobody knew who I was because I was completely covered up. I had to be careful to only dance as a raisin too. If I danced like I usually did, then people would know who I was- so, my act continued. It wasn't too long into the night when a good friend of mine asked me to dance. I had my best California Raisin dance going and he stopped me and laughed and said, "I am so sorry, but I just can't dance with a raisin." He had no idea who I was and I had to control my laughter. I also brought an oversized black lingerie because they were having a contest. At midnight, the contest was, 'The sexiest thing in black lingerie.' You got it, at midnight, I threw that thing on over my fat, plump purple raisin costume and had the entire place laughing.

For a time anyway, I was able to forget how heartbroken I was and really enjoyed being someone else that nobody knew.

I actually was having a great time being somewhere where my friends were but had no idea who I was the entire night. Until 'he' walked in with 'her.' My world stopped at that moment. They were arm-in-arm, and I froze for a minute. I could hear my heart beat and could not breathe. I decided I had to leave and I actually had to walk right past them to get to the door. I knew at that point, his plea to get the message to me to 'hang in there' was no longer true. And my tender heart was bruised all over again. I drove home once again crying. I could not wait to get out of my costume and cry the last cry I was going to allow with that rela-tionship.

Sometimes, you just have to pull yourself up any way that you can to regain who you are and decide to move forward.

I have seen so many people get stuck in the pain and never get over it, which is really bad for anyone. So, here are a few suggestions of things I have learned over the years to help you come back from a broken heart.

- There is nothing wrong with being sad. Cry if you need to, but try to limit your grief. You have too much life ahead of you. Of course, with timing, this completely depends on each situation.
- Figure out what you like to do, and do it.
- Seek out different places to go, not the places you went as a couple.
- Meet new people, and do new things.
- Smile, even though smiling is the last thing on your mind.

*H*ERE, HOLD MY WINE MOMENT:
I always smile through the pain. If you smile and make others happy, soon smiling will make you happy too. The song "Smile" comes to mind and comforts me when I need to get through a hard time. I hope it helps you too!

Chapter 12: Averett - Earning My BBA (Big, Bold Achievement) and MBA (Magnificent Bad Ass)

Stay with me here, the journey we are taking together is worth every minute you spend with me, I promise! When I think of a big bold move, I looked up what is the boldest, biggest wine and actually it is called a Douro Red. Douro Valley is in Portugal. According to what I have learned, you cannot even see through this wine.

FINALLY, MY SON WAS OLD ENOUGH AND I WAS READY TO GO back to school. I remember attending an informational meeting at Averett College and wondering if I was doing the right thing going back to school after so many years. This particular program was an accelerated program, meaning you do all of your classwork in five to eight weeks compared to the typical seventeen weeks.

I worried if I could do this demanding program and keep up with a demanding full-time job and be a single parent of a small child. I met the most wonderful woman at that informational meeting that night. I think we were both a bit scared at the thought of going back to school after so many years. We both wondered if we would even remember how to study, much less write papers and do presentations.

But I realize now the night I went to the meeting that this woman, who had two very small boys and a husband, would become someone with whom I would bond with very quickly. I honestly think that God, or my guardian angel, looks out for me and connects me to the right people when I need them the most. I honestly feel like she and I gave each other encouragement to move forward together. We have become someone we could each lean on and see if we could do this new type of learning together.

I remember the first night of class so clearly. We each had our chance to explain who we were and what we did for a living. Then we were asked to break off in groups of four and we would be together through that particular class.

My friend and I stuck together. Our first few 'group' people did not work out and we were able to switch people. Suddenly my friend and I had two other girls join our group and it was a match made in heaven. We quickly realized each of us had something to bring to the table. Where I was weak, someone else in our group was strong in that area. You get the idea! We were all honest about our capabilities and we all worked beautifully together. From that time on, our group flourished into fantastic students. We got the job done!! We were a feared group because we worked together so well. Our writing even became alike and when we worked on projects, things just seemed to pull together.

There were late nights, no doubt. Each person was in charge of writing certain sections. I would start papers. My friend would be one to make sure it made sense and pulled it all together. I felt bad for her because I think she had the hardest job and a lot of late nights.

For the most part, the four of us stayed together as a group, even though the college wanted us to shift to work with other people and rotate. We put our foot down and insisted we wanted to stay together as a team. Thankfully, the college allowed us to stay together.

We would also have to meet another night to work on our projects and ideas. We learned to 'speed read' to get through really large assignments that seemed impossible. We had to, at times, read eight chapters, after which we would each do the after-chapter questions on our own, write a paper on our own, find an article to share with the class, and explain what we read and understood for our article. Then we had a group project to present to the class. Each of us were responsible for putting our own slides together to go over our topic when presenting to the class. And we had to do all of this in a week. That is how fast and intense this accelerated program was for us having full time jobs and being moms as well.

I remember an assignment we had whereby we had to debate that women should not be paid as much as men in the workplace. Of course, we were highly upset with our topic to defend until we thought about it for a minute and decided to accept the challenge.

Suddenly, I was my mom. I dressed in an older type of dress, wore my hair up, and was the 'stay-at-home' mom who raised her children while her husband went to work. The other girls each dressed up as religious women of various faiths and expressed the belief that women would be the mother who stayed at home to rear the children and to 'keep the home fires burning,'

You know, I do remember growing up, and when I was in school and did not feel well, it was comforting to know my mom could be called. She would pick me up and she would be home with me to help nurse me back to health. There was a certain comfort to knowing no matter what, my mother would always be there for me.

So, we debated, in full-on dress 'garb,' and really threw off our competing team. They started laughing and could not hold their composure. Although our subject was difficult to defend, we did a great job and actually won the debate with how we approached the topic.

Later, we were tasked as a group to do what is called a SWOT analysis, which stands for: Strengths, Weakness, Opportunities, and Threats. We decided to do a SWOT analysis on Walmart. We asked for permission from Walmart to create a video at their store to discuss their background, how they operate as a company, and finalize a SWOT analysis. The Walmart spokesperson would not allow us to film inside, but allowed us to film outside.

We all decided to meet there in the same full 'garb' we wore during us defending that women should not get equal pay as men. Now we were going to Walmart as newly hired workers. While I was being filmed, it was pretty funny when an actual car that looked like the Beverly Hillbillies truck drove up and people that look like they had come directly out of the mountains jumped out of the vehicle and went inside of Walmart.

We took the opportunity to film me right in front of that truck. I said, "I am so excited because my kinfolk have come down today from the Mountains to do their shopping at Walmart." We all were giggling through the entire 'shoot' we were doing, and I adlibbed the dialogue, but it was perfect.

It was not long after we did the filming before the people came back, jumped in their dilapidated truck, and left.

Soon, it was another person's turn. She stood in front of the outdoor plants and with her eyes darting back and forth from left to right, she was telling a fact of how Walmart conducts business. We all laughed because it was so funny how she was trying to remember her lines and her eyes were all over the place.

Then the other girl was standing in front of a shopping cart. She said her lines on film and then suddenly, she said, "Hold on one minute, after all...it is my first day at work." So then she took the cart and put it in the cart holder in the parking lot. Again, we all broke out in laughter.

When it came time to be in the classroom to present, we showed the film and I swear, everyone, including us, was laughing until we all had tears running down our faces. Needless to say, our classmates loved the film and we got an 'A' on the project for being so creative. YAY!!!

One night, someone from another team spoke up and claimed our team was prejudiced. We all looked at each other with surprised faces, wondering why in the world anyone would come up with that idea. You see, we all looked at each other on our team as 'sisters.' However, my other three teammates were black and I am white. So, when we were forced to think about our dynamic, we had no idea why anyone was thinking saying we were prejudiced.

People try to do things to hurt each other with no need sometimes. Sometimes you just have to let people think what they want to think. As long as you are doing your best and making sure you have good intentions, doing what you can in life to get by at work, school and home, then you have to let those people think whatever they want and let them be to their own misery.

Our team stayed together, continued to blow away our school competition, and stayed the course. None of us see 'color' in each other. We see a lot of love, devotion and being sisters for life, as it should be.

After my BBA and MBA were completed at Averett University, I decided along with one of my teammates that we would go after our PhD together. Northeastern University had a program that one could do at home through video and by visiting the campus in Florida for two weeks.

The classes would be a bit challenging in that you had to go for two weeks wherever the professor taught somewhere in the United States. So, I would have had to take vacation, fly to the location and stay for two weeks.

In order to get accepted into the program, we both had to put together a portfolio of our business and academic achievements. We both submitted our best portfolio. I was accepted and she was not. Honestly, I believe I was accepted because my portfolio includes some very large business names and the University wanted someone with that type of exposure. However, she was and still is an exceptional person, and the University missed out on having a great, successful student.

I decided not to go because honestly, after doing the accelerated program for a duration of seven years with only a few months of rest, I was exhausted. Honestly, with the work that I do now, getting a PhD would not have done a lot more than my getting my Masters, so I decided to pass. And I really believe it was the right decision for me. My son was older now and need me to spend more time with him.

*H*ERE, HOLD MY WINE MOMENT:
Be bold...school is a fantastic thing you can do for you and your career. Nobody can ever take away your education.

Chapter 14: What It's Like Speaking for the First Time

I'm superstitious! NO CHAPTER 13! Speaking for the first time is like trying wine the first time. Doesn't always go well. But, you keep trying and finally, you will get it right!

~

I REALLY BELIEVE THAT WHEN MOST OF US THINK ABOUT PUBLIC speaking, we cringe at the thought of getting up in front of people to speak. I think speaking to people you know may be a bit easier, but speaking to a crowd of unknowns can even be more daunting.

My career in speaking started as a suggestion I made to my boss when others in the company were creating a lot of extra work in our department. I asked my boss if I could visit local company locations to see if I could make a difference.

I found myself with an overhead projector and a few slides I had made to go over the proper steps and procedures to ensure our processing in the department could be faster. As a result, I was able to give 'tips' to the travelers to make things go quicker in our department, resulting in our travelers getting any out-of-pocket expenses back in a timelier fashion.

I had to push myself based on a great cause for my department. I truly believe stepping out and doing something a little scary really helped propel my career. Next, I was volunteering to teach a class during a conference. The class had about fifty people in the room. The presentation was only an hour long, but I decided to pick a subject I knew a lot about. The room was filled with 'like' people in the same area of expertise I was in, so I brought an idea I created and implemented in my own company.

The crowd loved my ideas. After I spoke, people were grabbing my cards and asking me more questions as the session ended.

I really enjoyed bringing something to 'like' professionals, having them endorse what I was doing creatively, and having them using my ideas to help their company as well. After gaining the confidence I needed to speak in front of groups, I have now been asked to speak at as many as eight conferences in a year. It's nice when people come up to me afterwards; some even tell me I was the best speaker they heard at the conference.

$\mathcal{H}$ ERE, HOLD MY WINE MOMENT:

Don't think you can do a presentation in front of others? Go slow. Think about it, most of us are brought into meetings to sit around a big table and talk about issues or some other topic. It seems easier to talk when you are sitting around peers and voicing your opinion. You feel more comfortable because you know the people, you fully understand the issues, and you speak more freely. Graduate from there and make things a little harder next time. Perhaps stand when you are speaking your part at a meeting. By standing, you will be moving forward to feeling more comfortable with public speaking. Then keep going!

Chapter 15: Joy of Dancing

Life is a Cabernet, Old Friend!

∼

As my son grew up, I tried to do more things for myself that gave me a sense of happiness. When my son spent time with my parents, or was with my ex-husband or his family, I thought about something I enjoyed so much when I was growing up. Dance.

At five years old, my parents saw me dancing around to music in a very pretty slip that I thought was a princess dress. I would prance around in my white lace slip and my black patent leather shoes with little white anklet socks. My mother signed me up for ballet and tap. I ended up learning the art of dance for over fourteen years.

As I began my new journey through life, I heard about line dancing that seemed to be very popular at the time. I was going to school full-time in an accelerated program and I traveled for my work. I could not have had any more on my plate, plus I had a son to raise. However, I knew to keep my sanity I had to have an interest other than school, work, and my son.

One Thursday night after my 6 pm to 10 pm class, my baby sitter told me she would stay with my son and I should go dancing. So, I headed to a place called Dakotas. It was the peppiest country place I had ever been in before, but people were dancing to the tunes of a band and doing the two-step. The two-step is a couple's style of dance that people do to a certain country beat.

I had never done the two-step before, but with my ballet and tap dance background, I was able to quickly pick up the dance steps. Soon I had a real cowboy come over with his nicely pressed jeans, lightly scuffed cowboy boots, and his wide brimmed hat, asking me to dance.

I was hooked on the dancing, music, and laughter. I had so much fun that I realized this should be my outlet to relieve stress and build a new friendship base. It worked. Dancing to me was so stress relieving.

HERE, HOLD MY WINE MOMENT:

My days of dancing are long over. The knees and back do not want to cooperate so I am now in the pool. And I have made such great friends, and water exercise like HITT (High Intensity Training) and Tabata (an interval training) are great workouts. So at least I am still able to 'dance' (so to speak) to the music and the water routines. This type of exercise makes me really happy, and is really good for me too.

Chapter 16: Paymentech/JP Morgan Chase

It's always good to try something new! When you visit a winery, be sure to try all of their wines!

~

WHILE ATTENDING AVERETT UNIVERSITY, I HAD TO DO A research project in order to graduate. In doing my project, I was able to consult with a local company and save them ten million dollars in process savings! And I received an 'A' on my project!!

The company on which I did my research project, which was to help start a commercial card program, chose a firm that actually interviewed me for an implementation role. The card provider made me a fantastic offer and hired me!! Moving into a whole new industry was a complete risk. This was a card company that was brand new to the market, and I was about to leave a well-known fortune 500 company and twenty-one plus years of service.

I am sure you are wondering right now why anyone would leave a secure company for places unknown. For me,

I go with my gut instincts. When a decision feels right and you feel confident, go for it.

Do not be afraid of making a leap. I have known too many people who freeze when it comes time to make the move. Trust yourself, believe in yourself and do not look back. Remember, failure is not in your vocabulary!

As I ventured into the new world of commercial cards, it was a very exciting time in my life! I loved the people in the new company. Everything was totally different from anything I knew in the business world. Plus, I got to work out of my home and travel. How can you go wrong?

I knew I would be traveling a lot more than I did in my previous job. And, I continued with my Master's program and found myself doing homework on planes and in hotel rooms. To study is hard enough, but doing so in less than perfect conditions is not the easiest way to go. However, I was determined I was going to get everything done.

*H*ERE, HOLD MY WINE MOMENT: Don't ever be afraid to go into a different line of work. If you feel good about taking a chance and being a bit of a risk taker, then go for it. Making the move was the best move I ever made in my career and it can work for you too!

Chapter 17: New Job!

Never stay in one winery all day. Move on to new ones to expand your wine knowledge and palette.

❦

On to the new job and how I approached my new role. When starting with a new company, especially in a new industry, you have to prove yourself. I was now working for a bank after working in the manufacturing business for over twenty-one years.

I had a very kind mentor help me to 'learn the ropes,' so to speak. The mentor was my former account manager with whom I worked for my own card program at Reynolds Metals Company. It was nice to know someone I could trust. She actually went with me on my first several client onsite meetings.

I learned from her how to interact with clients. She taught me how to take the knowledge I had and come up with new ideas to help the clients succeed with their program. I absolutely loved the new role and before long, I realized I really had something to bring to the table to this new job. Once I started applying what I knew from my Reynolds Metals jobs, I was actually contributing something the card provider had not seen before. I was relatable to the client to whom we were trying to sell, and it helped us sell our products with a new twist, which included me and a consultative approach to selling.

I quickly became a favorite of several on the sales team since I had been a previous client, and I was familiar with the environment and people to whom they were selling, such as Accounts Payable, Purchasing and Travel. I soon became the resident expert when dealing with client issues. I loved to understand each client and their unique situations. I recognized their specific cultures and what they could and could not do.

*H*ERE, HOLD MY WINE MOMENT:
Never underestimate the power of the knowledge you have and use it in your new position. Draw on past experiences if you can and build your confidence!

Chapter 18: My Story from 9/11 - "Gimme the Gun!"

I think this job is for a really strong and bold Wine... LET'S GO with a Norton (Virginia grape) for this one!

I FLEW INTO SYRACUSE, NEW YORK ON SEPTEMBER 10, 2001. I was going to meet a coworker I had never met before. He told me not to worry about renting a car. He was from New York and stated he would meet me at the hotel. We would go out to dinner that evening and then in the morning, we would go together to visit the client for our meeting. Then he would drop me off at the airport.

However, I felt more comfortable not being left without a vehicle, so I rented a car anyway. Little did I know, it would be the best decision I could have made on this trip!

We went to dinner that night and then I followed him the next day to meet with Carrier Corporation in time for our 9 am meeting on September 11th. Of course, none of us had any idea what was about to happen not too far away from where we were.

At about 8:45 am, people were walking into the conference room. My coworker's phone rang and it was his wife. He picked up his phone and said, repeating her words as a question, "A plane just hit the World Trade Center?" None of us thought it was anything more than a small plane and a freak accident. We went on with our meeting, not realizing the tragedy that was unfolding.

Two hours later, we opened the door to the conference room and saw people were running by the room. I looked at the Carrier guy next to me and asked if possibly we missed a fire drill exercise. He said he felt we would have heard the alarm.

So we all walked the same way people were scurrying out and there were three TVs set up. By then, we started hearing the horrific attack on the World Trade Center. By the time we saw what was going on, the Pentagon had also been hit. My co-worker immediately tried calling his wife back, but by then the cell towers were down and cell service was not available. Unfortunately, his wife worked at a building next to the World Trade Center. You could see the blood drain out of his face when he realized she was in trouble.

I called my mother who was frantic, and told her I would be driving home. She wanted me to leave that moment, but I had already promised to take the client to lunch before I left for the day. My co-worker headed out, trying to get home and to make sure his wife was okay. Luckily that day she was one of the lucky people who made it out of downtown Manhattan.

I took the client to an Italian place and we were the only customers there that day. Normally I would have a pretty nice car, but I actually had a small Ford Escort of all things. The two guys jumped in the car and the guy in the front said, "This thing sounds like a truck." We all laughed. I think that was the only time I laughed that day.

Obviously, the impact was so devastating the world actually stopped that day. After I dropped my client off back at their office, I changed clothes quickly out of my suit and started driving all the way back to Virginia.

I was extremely happy I had the rental car or I would have been stuck since air traffic was not allowed for a week after the attacks.

That trip was the longest ride I ever had, driving all the way back to Virginia. When going past Scranton, Pennsylvania, I could see the smoke from the flight that went down in nearby Shanksville as part of the attacks that day.

The entire trip was filled with a radio with no music. Instead there was commentary as things were happening at Ground Zero and other attacked locations. It was a very sad ride listening to the desperation in people's voices as they talked about the events unfolding. In the background, I heard the beeping of the firefighter's jackets going off because of detectors designed to help locate them.

I would periodically call my mother, who lived with me at the time, to let her know where I was in my trip. I had left New York at 1:30 PM that day. After stopping one time quickly for gas and a snack, I arrive at 11 pm at home in Virginia. I got home in time to see the news. Back then, the replay was of people literally jumping to their death to get away from the flames and smoke. Truly it was a heartbreaking event to watch.

I remember trying to work that week. Even though I was at home, several of my coworkers were stuck for a week in hotel rooms. I remember trying to work, but I just didn't have it in me. Obviously, the events of that week really got to me. I was so sad and hurt by what happened. All I could think about were all of the lives lost and the non-stop view of Ground Zero, the smoke coming up from Shanksville, and the big gaping hole in the Pentagon.

It was a time the nation needed to heal. For the first time in a long time, I could see people being kind to one another. We all had those magnetic flags we put on our cars to show our support and to send a message that we were the USA and nobody would attack us like this again.

I sometimes feel we are so divided as a nation and wish we could get back to a time when we all banded together as one. Let's all make an effort to remember the lessons of 9/11 and come together again.

I remember my first trip about a week after 9/11. I had to fly directly into New York City's LaGuardia airport. I had a seat up in first class for a change. Across the aisle from me was a TSA agent. Back when 9/11 first happened, the agents were actually in uniform.

The poor guy apparently had never flown before. He looked terrified when the plane took off and especially when we hit turbulence for the first time. I looked over at him and said, "Don't worry, that was just turbulence and is very normal." He thanked me and seemed to be a bit more at ease at that point.

When we were ready to land, I felt like I had to tell the poor guy to expect when we landed at the airport. It is a very short runway and the pilot puts the brakes on pretty hard. He was very thankful I told him so he knew what to expect and that it was okay. I felt like I was the one that should have had the gun to protect everyone. I have a feeling if anything did happen, I would have had to take over to help the poor guy!

I had to stay the night, so I booked a hotel from where I could easily walk to the office. But the hotel had just reopened. I did not think about it, but the hotel was right across the street from Ground Zero. I had heard people talking about being at the site of the 9/11 disaster and that it was very strange. They said they could feel the souls who had passed away during that fateful day.

When I realized where my hotel was that night, I thought about having to see the destruction left behind and wondered how I would feel about being there. I decided to have breakfast at the hotel that morning before I walked to work. I could see the workers who were working on cleaning up the devastation.

After breakfast, I walked out of the front door and immediately was overwhelmed. I felt sadness, I felt terror, and I could feel the souls. The feeling was so powerful I was taken aback.

I quickly left that area, but as I walked, I could not shake the feeling that seemed to consume me. It really made me realize what horror happened that day. I have since been back to see the memorial. I would hope everyone will consider going to the memorial and never forgetting what happened that day as it is certainly well worth seeing.

To this day, that guy in the front seat of the car from the client office and I call each other each anniversary to touch base. We are 9/11 buddies. When you share a day like that with someone, you never forget that day, who you were with and how you felt.

HERE, HOLD MY WINE MOMENT:

September 11, 2001 is a day we should all remember. If you were not born yet when it occurred, please take time to learn about that day. And let's remember why it is important to fight for our freedom. Thank our military for keeping us safe and allowing us to be free.

Chapter 19: Good Customer Service

In any business, even wineries, bad customer service can bury you. If someone treats you with respect, makes you feel important and listens to you, the business will be a success!

～

THE BEST ADVICE I CAN EVER GIVE SOMEONE IS TO LEARN TO become a good listener. Repeat what you have heard and make sure you have a full understanding of the client's needs, issues, and goals.

I can honestly say I have implemented hundreds of clients in my work career and no two clients are the same. Clients can be in the same industry and even have the same Enterprise Resource Planning (ERP) systems, but may still have very different cultures and use the systems differently.

When working in a customer-focused job, you need to put yourself in their position. If something happens and your client is upset, you have to approach them with a sense of urgency, empathy, and understanding.

I have been a client before and I can tell you the worst thing that can happen is to ignore their issues. You first should contact them and let them know you are working on the issue. Make sure you have clarity of exactly what the issue may be and solve for this issue. Let them know you will get back to them with updates, and do consider their issue critical.

Sometimes you have to admit that you or your company made an error. Never try to cover up an issue. If you have to smooth things over, you can come up with something reasonable, but be honest. Clients are a lot more forgiving when you:

1. Admit the error.

2. Let them know you are actively working on correcting the issue.

3. Map out for them when the error will be corrected.

If you inform a client that you will get back with them by the end-of-the-day with an answer, let them know you are touching base with them; even if you do not have an answer yet the issue is still being resolved. Clients appreciate when someone keeps their word, and are more forgiving when they know you are actively keeping them abreast of the resolve and timing.

I will never forget a client I had in Chicago. The sales-person had sold a travel expense reporting tool to the client and I found out right before I went in to have the implementation kick-off that our company created a 'stop sell' for that product. A stop sell is what it says. The product is not working, we could no longer sell and implement that product, and it was pulled from our company as an offering.

I was sitting in front of approximately twenty people with a coworker, and we had to decide what to do. The group was very upset learning that even though they had signed a contract for the travel tool, they would not be able to use that process. I knew they now had the ability to cancel their contract, so it was up to us to save the client.

Here's how we I decided to make a difference. We ended up using the regular purchasing tool we had in place by suggesting we create travel categories as drop-down menus, and made it a 'point-and-click' way for the client to categorize their travel selections. This was not typically a functionality of a purchasing card tool.

We also worked with their technical team and created an 'out-of-pocket' link so a spreadsheet could be filled out for the cash expenses (these are expenses for which travelers pay cash and need to be reimbursed). The idea was to 'net' the expenses of the company charged to the card, and the cash that was owed to the cardholder. We would route via the clients' intranet. The solution helped save the client time and money by adding the cash due as a non-taxable line to the cardholder's payroll.

By adding reimbursement to the payroll, checks were eliminated if written in the past. An ACH io Automated Clearing House – it is an electronic payment. An example, when you set up bill pay, some of those to pay your bill goes directly from your account to the bank account of the payee and deposited directly into their account. If the funds were sent directly to the bank via ACH, they would save the cost of the ACH and gain some float by paying out the funds when payroll usually processed.

Luckily, the solution I mentioned worked and the client stayed with our company. The idea was one we used with future clients and it worked beautifully.

*H*ERE, HOLD MY WINE MOMENT:
Think 'out-of-the-box,' and you too will be surprised how you can save your company or other companies money and/or time.

Chapter 20: Creative Solutions at Work

A Pinot Noir Sparkling is a great solution to appeal to those who love red wine and then expand their dynamics to appeal to a larger group of wine connoisseurs!

COMING UP WITH CREATIVE SOLUTIONS IS WHAT PROPELLED MY career. I know many of you have thought of better ways to do things and just never thought about either putting it in place as a new practice, or promoting your idea to other companies. You should promote your ideas! That is how I made a name for myself, and you can too!

I want to share an example with you. I was implementing new cards at a very large university in the Chicago area. It was time for us to order their cards. We overnighted the cards to the program administrator because we really needed the client to get their cards as promised on time. Wouldn't you know it, the cards did not make the deadline!

When the program administrator called me and told me the cards did not show up, I looked up the overnight number. Even though our bank had entered the correct address on the package, it was delivered to the wrong company. Really? "Why me?" I thought.

So, I had to get our Operations group to send new cards to them and they were promised this time for a Saturday delivery. The program administrator came all the way from her home in the suburbs of Chicago to the city to get the cards. I received a call that Saturday afternoon and learned the cards never arrived. I was about to die at this point.

Later I found out that after several attempts to get the client their cards, the overnight delivery service had delivered the cards to the wrong company once again. Really? Lovely!! Even though it was another company's fault, you have to be the one to ensure the issue is corrected. You cannot just pass it off even though another company was in error.

*H*ERE, HOLD MY WINE MOMENT:
Remember, in your career, things are going to happen that are not so pleasant. However, it is how you recover that is most important. Be diligent and expect your business partners stay on top of things as well.

Chapter 21: How I Knocked Out the New York Execs with a Good Presentation

My 'knock-out' wine is a Pollak Vineyard 2009 Cabernet Sauvignon. Pollak is a Virginia vineyard and had a fantastic winemaker there. Worth the visit!

Take the word from someone who has dealt with mishaps more than I would like to admit: unless someone's life is in danger, you can work through anything. Keep a cool head, think it through, create a plan to recover, and communicate.

Several years had gone by and our company was doing so well that Paymentech was bought by JPMorgan Chase. I was asked to present to the top executives at an off-site meeting. I thought of something about which I felt passionate, so I chose the topic 'Understanding Your Client.'

The executives were from New York on Wall Street. I know that most of you would die thinking about doing a presentation for executives; however, in this industry, it is commonplace to talk to client executives. Plus, I was going to school and every night of our class, we had to speak about topics we had to research for understanding and then present.

I did not have much time, so I created a presentation in the matter of a few minutes. I decided how I wanted to approach the topic. Once you decide what you want to present, then you can easily put your ideas into slides. Always keep in mind who you are presenting to and the message you want to get across to them.

Some tips I would like to share about presentations:

- Do not put your presentation word-for-word on a PowerPoint slide. Just use bullet points with ideas to prompt you for what you want to say. The more words you put on a slide, the quicker you will lose people's attention. People want to hear your thoughts expressed naturally, and not read what you have written on a PowerPoint slide.
- Also, do not use aids such as 3x5 cards or notes of any kind. In order to sound credible, know what you want to say and ensure your bullets simply help you keep your thoughts in order. As you are presenting, always look for understanding from your audience.
- If your audience members look like 'deer in the headlights,' then ask if everyone understands the points you have gone over. Hopefully, those who have questions will ask for clarification. If they ask, be prepared to explain a point a different way to help get your point across.
- Sometimes, an audience will be quiet and not ask questions. Be sure to engage your audience. Get them to feel free to ask questions and possibly create questions for them to become part of your presentation.

- I am not one to practice before a presentation. I know most of you would cringe at the thought of presenting without practicing, but everyone has their own comfort zone. I am much better when I do not practice. Have you even had someone go over a presentation and say to you, "remember to say this..."? Or, "make sure you don't say that..." Nothing will get you off track quicker than trying to remember those points.

After the presentation, one of the New York executives came up to me and actually said, "That was the best presentation I have ever seen." I was absolutely shocked because I put the slides together so quickly. At first, I thought she was joking with me because, after all, she was from Wall Street and I knew she must have seen fantastic presentations.

But then I realized it was the concept I used in the presentation that she liked. Most companies seem to pass over the point I was trying to make. And my concept was about how to communicate with the various areas of a company that our product will either help or change how they are doing things today.

I believe the 'light bulb' came on with her because of our mindset of having a product and convincing a client it's the greatest technology. If you were a really good sales person, you could work your 'magic' to show clients the 'bells and whistles' of the tool that would make the client want the product.

My vision, and what I have always preached is, you have to really understand what the client's business is and how they run their operations. Understanding not only that each industry is different but also within the same industry that each client may do things very differently makes the differ-

ence. You cannot just sell a client a product without reall
understanding their needs and how what you are selling
can help them to make things better in their company.

The executive asked me what my role was at
the company, and I explained to her that I was
an implementer of card products. She stated she
thought I was very smart and she was going to
create new positions. She said she hoped that I would
look over the positions and consider posting for one that
interested me.

Not too long after that conversation, she had posted
newly created positions and one was the manager of the
East Coast implementers. I applied for the manager's position and after the interview process, the position was offered
to me. I was thrilled because I was able to get back into
management with the new position.

I love being a manager because I have always worked
very hard to make things better for those who report to me. I
usually am in a position whereby I know the work because I
have done the job of those I am managing. So when
someone on my team talks about an issue, I can fully understand what they are talking about, and can help figure out
how to make the process better.

The difference in the position I had taken was that
former peers were now reporting to me. So, you can imagine
the hard feelings people had with me getting the job when
they did not. And, in many cases, the people now reporting
to me had been with the company far longer than I had.

It took time, but each person on the team learned I was
prepared to make things better for them and for their
respective clients. Everyone at that point started to open up
and trust me (thankfully). I took the approach of not being
the one who makes the decision, but determined it was up
to all of us on the team to make the decision. I was simply

the person who would go up to management to help make changes for the better. Although decisions were supported by team, if people on the team were at odds, I would be the final decision maker.

ℋERE, HOLD MY WINE MOMENT:

Our team quickly became the number one team for JPMorgan Chase. I encouraged each person to make decisions, and no matter what, I would back anyone on my team. Empowering employees shows that you trust them, but more importantly, you have to stand by them, right or wrong.

Chapter 22: Presenting about Fraud

Avoid bad wine! Go directly to your chosen winery and get the facts from the experts. Don't be afraid to taste and learn about the wines and figure out what you like and do not like. I hate to say that there are not many I do not like!

ANOTHER TIME I PRESENTED WAS WHEN I WAS ASKED TO SPEAK at a conference about fraud in Las Vegas. Now get this one, because I thought this was a set-up. I received a call with the caller ID showing my company's name. I answered it, and this guy tells me he is from our events group (which we do have) and said because I was a speaker, they could get me a lower rate. I said that was great, so he transferred me to the hotel to 'be sure I got the new rate.'

A guy answered and said I could go from the $285.00 per night rate to $199.00 rate and I could even extend before the conference and after since I was a speaker. I said that sounded great. So, then he said he would send me an e-mail. I figured it would be great if I decided to go in early and/or stay late in Vegas!

So I waited with him on the phone to see if I received my e-mail. I received it and he told me I needed to confirm by clicking into the IDOCS button. That is when my red flag went up on the side of my head. I knew something was not right. He kept telling me to click on the button and I was e-mailing the conference people waiting for an answer if this was a scam.

They did not get back with me, so I just told him I would have to do this transaction later because my boss was calling and we had a client issue we had to deal with immediately.

The next day, the conference group I was speaking for said it was a scam and was getting immediately to their lawyers to handle the issue.

Those two guys tried calling me back several times and I ignored them. I also let my company know the scam that was being pulled so they could warn others. It really makes me mad because they take billions of dollars every year from defrauding good people.

So you can imagine how I started my conference session. I said I wondered if I was asked to speak about fraud and that was a set-up they did to test me. When I asked if anyone else in the room was a conference speaker and nobody raised their hand, so I said, "So, I got it now, it WAS a set up." They all started laughing.

$\mathcal{H}$ ERE, HOLD MY WINE MOMENT:
Sometimes when you speak, a good solid attention-getter at the beginning will get them to listen to your message.

Chapter 23: Changes At Work

Hang in here with me....this one is really hard and pivotal to decisions I had to make. I think another strong wine is in order....let's see....Take This Job and Shiraz It!

I WAS THE MANAGER OF THE EAST COAST IMPLEMENTERS FOR A short time when a Vice President position came open. The new job was to be in charge of all of the United States implementation teams. I did not know if I would be considered, but thought I would apply. When I was actually chosen for the position, I was so excited because I felt as though I finally made a name for myself. My 'brand' was recognized by upper management. I had a chance now to really make a difference.

I had been in my new role as VP of the Program Consulting group for JPMorgan Chase for only four months when my boss interrupted a meeting I was conducting. I happened to be in our office location in Salt Lake City for the week to complete year-end appraisals for people on my team. The boss announced that JPMorgan was now buying

Bank One. My first reaction was wondering how many card conversions my team would have to add to our already busy schedule.

Typically, when one company acquires another company, the company making the purchase will give the new company a piece of the business to run. This company purchase was no different, and it was not long when we learned Bank One's management team was taking over commercial cards. And that was the group that I worked for at the time.

The interesting part about Bank One taking over is that I had interviewed with them about six months prior to this acquisition. And, needless to say, when the guy who had interviewed me, whom I had turned down, walked through the door and said, "Well, Robin Anderson, I see we had to take over in order to get you," I knew at that moment it may not be good for me.

My job now at JPMorgan Chase was a duplicate of a job that belonged to someone else he had working for him. I knew I would not have my new job for long; however, Bank One's top executive stated that anyone who was appointed to be on the merger team would be considered their top employees, and would be guaranteed a job once the merger tasks were completed.

So, as I guessed, the other person took my job. My heart was broken because I had worked so hard to finally get the job of my dreams. But, I knew I needed to go this path for some reason. I was appointed to a team reporting to an incoming Bank One person and helped decide how all of the conversions would be done. I was now on the merger team, was considered a top employee, and was guaranteed a job.

It was a pretty complicated process because not only were we converting all of their portfolios to

JPMorgan Chase's card application, but a decision was made to use the processor that Bank One used. I know this seems confusing, but to explain at a very high level, there are only a few card processors in the entire card world. Each processor is different in many ways. Changing a client from one processor to the other may sound easy, but it creates a lot of steps to implement each client, and the setup was so differ-ent, you could not just convert the existing program as it was currently running.

Our team would meet several times every few months and work on various things needed to get a plan together to convert clients. We were trying to combine documents that JPMorgan and Bank One respectfully had to simplify the upcoming tasks.

I had mentioned that a certain document would not be easy to combine into one because of the two systems being so different. I suggested that we wait to combine much later when we were able to convert clients. Doing so would be less confusing to the implementation team.

When I made the suggestion, two others apparently felt I was trying to tell them what to do, and they shut me down very quickly. So I asked some of the others on the team who seemed to agree with me what I was missing. They all agreed I had the right idea.

The next onsite meeting we had, one of the two said she had a great idea. So the boss (who was the other person agreeing with her, not me) said, "I have a great idea." The boss said, "What is your idea?" And she went on to say, "I think because the tools are different, we need to keep the two forms until we get some clients implemented." She had just said what I said the last time we were all together. And their acting job was horrible. You could tell the conversation was rehearsed, and it was like watching a really bad porn movie.

My coworkers who had agreed with me looked at me in astonishment. I could not contain myself and I stated, "Well, I wonder where you got that idea from?" Needless to say, the 'boss' thought her idea was brilliant. I was fuming. I was so upset that I had an immediate nose bleed because my blood pressure shot up so quickly, and I had to go out of the room. Not a good thing, but I did have to walk out for obvious reasons.

I knocked on the door of our Human Resources (HR) person, and he looked up when I said, "I am going to kill someone." And he replied saying, "Come in and shut the door." This was some years ago, and now if you said what I did, they probably would have the SWAT team there in 20 seconds or less, but I had to get it off of my chest.

In all my years of working in the business world, I had never been treated with such disrespect. The HR guy told me that the new company employees had been treating everyone badly and what I was experiencing was happening to a lot of heritage JPMorgan Chase people. It was a very sad time because we had such a wonderful team. Everyone got along so great, and, we were able to build our card group from fifteen people when I walked into the door to hundreds of people within just a few years. We were very successful.

To make matters worse, the Bank One guy who told us anyone on the merger teams would be guaranteed a job was let go from his duties. Then we were told that we each had to find our own jobs once the merger duties were complete.

So, I called a few people in our card world and Treasury for JPMorgan Chase to see if I could secure employment, but people were not stepping up to open jobs. So I decided I had better look outside of JPMorgan Chase.

*H*ERE, HOLD MY WINE MOMENT:

Have you ever felt at some point at work that you were no longer appreciated? Well, you are not alone. Typically, the number one reason people leave a job is that they do not feel valued. I have seen many brilliant ideas by staff members only to have a boss take all of the credit and present it as their own. I have also seen goal setting, policy and procedures put in place that bypass what is right for the client and puts some departments at odds.

I have also seen when people would do whatever they had to do to reach their goal, even if it meant another person would not meet their goal. So let's take these common problems in the workplace today and come up with some ideas of how to overcome the pending issues.

Chapter 24: Find a Job Before You Leave a Job

Be Bold, Be a Nice Burgundy from France – Called 'Pinot Noir' in the United States!

I was promoted to VP of Merger of Implementations. I was now a peer of the guy who previously was my boss, and he did not like that I was now equal to him. I was enjoying a little bit of his jealousy, to be honest.

A good friend of mine had called me and stated there was a director's position open at American Express. He called the hiring manager and got my résumé in front of her. Soon I was called for an interview. I flew into New York City to the American Express headquarters and I interviewed with several executives there.

The last step of the process was for me to put together a 15-minute presentation and describe to them what I felt the future of the card would look like in the next five years. As I shared earlier, doing this kind of presentation was right up my alley. I enjoy being creative.

I presented to several people. I completed the presentation in exactly fifteen minutes and the hiring leader said, "I can't believe you did that in exactly fifteen minutes." I got the job.

I successfully made the move from JPMorgan to American Express as Director of Implementation. It was not often that American Express actually hired from the outside of their firm.

I did the usual protocol, calling and meeting with my peers and my specific team members. However, a very unusual set of circumstances happened to bring about a very different way to gain trust and respect with my team.

I was not with American Express very long when one of my team members called to tell me he was having medical issues with his back. He stated he had rods put in his back several years before and he felt something had slipped that was causing him pain.

A visit to his doctor produced the usual, 'go home, rest and take these medications, and your pain will go away' type of visit. However, one Sunday evening not long after the doctor visit, his wife called me to explain she had to call the rescue squad to take him to the hospital because he was in so much pain.

I made sure any calls he had for the next few days were covered. I worried he was going to be out for some length of time for back surgery. He called me the next morning and explained they found out that he had broken his hip and the hip was the cause his pain.

I called a team meeting and explained his situation and that we needed to all cover for him while he recuperated. The team was great and everyone pulled together to step in and ensure his duties were covered. The team effort helped us to all get closer as a group.

The very next day, he called me and told me he had been diagnosed with stage 4 lung cancer. I thought he was joking with me. Unfortunately, he was not. This man, who never smoked and never even ate bad things like most of us do, was suddenly in the fight for his life. His situation made me wonder how in the world this can happen to someone who lives such a clean life. I was stunned, and so was the team.

He called me after the shock wore off and stated he was committed to fighting as hard as he could. He begged me to allow him to keep his job since he had a wife and two twin daughters to support. Since our jobs called for about 60% of our time traveling to meet clients, I went to my boss to make a case to the HR department to allow him to continue to work. They granted our wish.

He immediately had to receive radiation and chemo-therapy. The next time I saw him was during an offsite meeting in his hometown. He came to the meeting for lunch with myself and another person from my team. We were shocked at his appearance. He was walking with a cane from the broken hip and his formerly full head of dark hair was now only a few sprigs of grey on a much balder head on top of a very frail body. He appeared to go from the age of 48 to 98 in the matter of a few months.

All who saw him that day were in complete shock. We all did our best to put smiles on our face and try to give posi-tive words to this man who was going through the battle of his life. It was the hardest day I think I have ever had to endure. But, just think how hard the day was for him to face all of his work friends in such a deteriorated state.

About six months had passed and he was still enduring the cocktail of drugs with chemo and having some issues with memory, which is common with cancer patients. He was still working and taking calls. I did receive a call from a client complaining she could not understand why he could not come to see her on-site.

I explained to her in confidence of his pending fate and then she was a lot more understanding. I told her I would come and visit her. I told him that his client was upset and he stated he would get permission from his doctor and would come as well.

At the time, I was having my house painted. I had two new lab puppies. When the painters took a break, I let the puppies outside to stretch their legs. Of course they wanted to jump in the van with the painters and share their lunches! However, the painters were not really happy with that visit. So, I grabbed the puppies' collars and led them over to the grass.

Suddenly, they both took off running- I assume to chase a squirrel- and I was sent sliding across the concrete sidewalk with my face. I put Neosporin all over my wounds and then the next day, my eyes were swelling shut. I went to see my regular doctor who then sent me to the emergency room since I had to fly the next day to see the client.

The ER doctor walked in and unfortunately for me, the Neosporin looked like pus on my face. Of course, standing before me had to be the most handsome man I had ever seen. The handsome doctor did give me the green light to travel after several x-rays, so I flew to Atlanta. First, I met my team member with cancer and we flew to Oklahoma together. We were a pair, me with my 'pus' looking face and he with his bald head and cane to help him walk.

We arrived to the hotel and had plans the next day to meet up with two local American Express people to go with us to see the client. That morning, we had a tornado hit and did not have power. Luckily, I was able to grab shower before the tornado hit but had not dried my hair. I also could not use the curling iron to get the frizzes out of my hair either. My face by now was all scabs. Not a great look.

When we met the two from American Express, whom

we had never met in person before, I thought they were going to hit the floor. Can you imagine how they felt when they saw a bald man with a cane that looked 100 years old and a blonde girl with big frizzy hair with scabs on her face? It was pretty funny!

Meeting the client was funny as well for us to see their expressions. We just explained our issues of why we looked the way we did and continued with the meeting. That day, we earned a lot of respect for each other and our team and the client respected us as well.

Our coworker managed to fight for two years before he succumbed to the cancer in the month of November. Even though he was unable to work to the required date of February 1st to be able to qualify for his annual bonus, my boss presented his widow with his bonus check. To me, that shows respect for a fallen coworker. I was grateful I worked for such a great company.

$\mathcal{H}$ERE, HOLD MY WINE MOMENT:

There comes a time in a manager's life when you have to put aside what the company may think is right and you need to be empathetic to people who work for you. Everyone has a life outside of work. Know each one of your employees. If you can help them in any way, do it! It's the right thing to do!

SPECIAL HAPPY HOUR MOMENT:

GOAL SETTING

A lot of companies have goals for each person driven down from the top leadership. Each group or division is responsible for a certain amount of the overall goal to contribute to the ultimate company goal.

Each person ends up with a goal to show expectations of performance each year: however, if goals are not thought out properly by a company, the results can be devastating.

Each group has to figure out how to create measurable goals and push them down to each employee. Sounds fair: however, for groups who overlap and depend on the other to obtain goals, this can sometimes be challenging when alignment does not happen between the two groups.

For example, say each sales person has a goal to sell $30 million within a year timeframe. When the goal is set, you have each sales person signing deals that are possibly overstating the volume expected for the client.

The team and/or person who is then responsible to ensure the client is implemented and achieves that goal realizes the client will only do $15 million. (When I say "the client is implemented" I mean we take all of the steps over months to build their program and get cards out to them.

Once that happens, we watch the volume charged on those cards and everyone is measured on that volume.) The sales person meets their goal because they signed the deal and got the client to agree but the person implementing is told it was their fault the client did not reach its goal.

I have also seen where the sales team is in charge of getting not only new clients but also working with an existing client to get a new product into the client's portfolio and get more volume. However, you have a Relationship Account Manager (RAM) who owns the relationship.

The RAM is in charge of getting volume also on each account in their portfolio, and the salesperson and RAM cannot both claim the sale. So, you have a conflict between the Sales and the RAM team. And, you can imagine how these groups are at odds all the time.

Companies really have to think through goal setting in a more logical way. I have seen whereby people were let go from a company because a client left the company for a competitor.

The RAM is responsible for each client, regardless of the reason why the client left.

However, if a client leaves the company, it is very possible it was not the RAM's fault and, there needs to be a way for a judgement be given, and not fire someone just because the client severed the relationship.

My team fought for a change to the rules. It was decided finally when it came to Sales signing a client's volume worth, an alignment was required between the Sales person and the implementer to agree. By establishing this alignment, the new processes created teamwork.

This new rule did help keep the sale in a more realistic scenario. Likewise, sales could only be brought into an existing client when there was a competitive bid which would require the expertise of a sales associate. Again, this created a team effort.

I remember one time when a new leader took over our group. She was younger, and I guess had a lot to prove. She asked all who reported to her for ideas on how to make some changes. Each of us gave ideas that were totally discounted.

When she came back and did not take in to account anything her team suggested, she decided to change me and my team from client facing to a project management team only. I knew I would never get the opportunity to do what I did best, which was to work with the client face-to-face to help build a fantastic program.

The day I told her I was taking a new job with a competitor and that I was going to miss being in front of the client with the change she made in my position, she stated to me, "Well, I guess you better dust off those suits." I realized at that moment that moving on was the right thing for me.

*H*ERE, HOLD MY WINE MOMENT:
To sum up the importance of you finding your balance and what makes you happy, below is a great quote I came across recently. I do not know who wrote it but thought it was perfect for this chapter.

"In case you forgot to remind yourself this morning – your butt is perfect. Your smile lights up the room. Your mind is insanely cool. You are way more than enough. AND, you are doing an amazing job at life."

Take control of your happiness. I did and I never look behind me. You can too!!

Chapter 25: When You Drink Too Much, Sometimes You Step Sideways!

I'm not calling any names here, but I have one friend who had a little too much Blueberry Wine and still cannot remember much about that evening!

∾

Leaving American Express was a big change for me. When you make a change, you always hope the next move is a good one for your career. Sometimes, you have to be a risk taker to move up in life.

When I interviewed with SunTrust Bank, the person I would work for was very convincing. The hiring manager stated I would start off as an individual contributor and would not take long for me to move back into management with my background.

Honestly, after being in management for so long, the thought of getting back to being responsible for only me was a welcome thought for the short term. Since the other bank was unable to make a decision at the time, I accepted the SunTrust position as a Program Officer of the bank. I was quickly given about thirty clients to manage and visit onsite. I was surprised at the number of clients I was given. Typically, you do not handle more than twenty clients to effectively service.

I started to see my clients one by one. I realized that a lot of clients were never implemented correctly. I had to have day-long meetings to figure out from each client what was not working for them and basically redesign their whole programs.

The redesigns took time and it took a while before I could position my clients to trust again to achieve my goal, to increase their spend dollars.

When clients are not happy or the program is not working for them, you have to take a step back and fix the issues before you can ask a client to look at other products. Before I knew it, I was assigned over the course of a year with seventy-plus clients.

In order to keep up, I worked at least twelve hours a day and a lot of time on the weekends. But, I did keep up with my clients and was getting a lot of great feedback to my manager about my work and commitment.

*H*ERE, HOLD MY WINE MOMENT:
Do not ever think you cannot take a step back. Expanding your résumé with a new area of expertise can still be a great career move.

Everyone has a job from time-to-time where the conditions may not be easy. Take those challenges as your catalyst to prove you can do whatever is thrown at you. Never give up! Instead, prove you can do the job and eventually, good things will happen for you.

Chapter 26: When Opportunity Comes Calling, What Will YOU Do?

Go ahead, take a risk. Try a new wine. How about a nice Pinot Grigio? Just so you know, a Pinot Gris is actually the same grape with a different name!

After about fourteen months of working for SunTrust, I received a call from that company I had interviewed with prior to taking the SunTrust job; however, there was an opportunity at SunTrust to be the manager of the group and I was asked to interview for the position.

I had one last onsite with SunTrust Bank before I made my decision. During this period of time in Atlanta, Georgia, there was a snow storm that crippled the city.

Luckily, as we left the office, we were able to catch the Metropolitan Atlanta Rapid Transit Authority (MARTA). We had to wait a very long time in frigid cold because many of the train tracks had been shut down due to the weather-related issues.

We finally got to our hotel, dragging our luggage in unprepared clothing, shoes slipping on the ice. We were fortunate to be staying at the Ritz Carlton Hotel, which was not too bad but proved to be very expensive for SunTrust.

I remember waking up the next morning and everything seemed to be so quiet. I looked out of the window and the scene was very, very strange to me. Here I was in downtown Atlanta and there was nothing moving. No cars, no police, no rescue squads, and no people walking.

It may sound really funny but I thought I died overnight and this is what you experienced when you were dead. Don't laugh at me but really! And unless you know what the experience is, how do we really know, right?

Luckily, my cell phone rang and it was my neighbor from home calling to see if I was okay. I thanked her for calling me and explained what I saw outside or did not see to be more exact. I told her I thought I was dead and needless to say, hearing her laugh so hard made me feel better that I truly was alive!

While in Atlanta, I had an interview with my boss, and he stated I was a top candidate. The next step was to inter-view with his boss. When we were stranded, the big boss had the opportunity to speak with me, but he did not. I knew then he had no intent to consider me for the role. So, my decision was easily made on my next steps with my next career move.

When I gave my notice, a lot of the clients and fellow employees were very upset SunTrust was not able to keep me. As a matter of fact, I found out from a close friend that the head of the department (my boss' boss) stated I set expectations too high with clients and the Treasury bankers for SunTrust whom I worked closely with to manage clients.

You know what? I will take that compliment. Everyone needs to make sure your clients are happy. And at the end of the day, my clients were poised to start spending more. I was satisfied I had done my job! I let my clients be my validation even though I was not given any praise from my management.

The new company with whom I was starting had a new card product, and I was hired because of my expertise. Finally, I could use all of my years of experience in business, my specific knowledge of accounts payable, travel, and purchasing, while also using my education to help design the best processes for our clients.

I love being in front of the client, helping get the sale, and designing each and every client's program. A lot of other companies do not listen to clients. They just put in a canned product and a check-list type of implementation. Since I used to be a client, I know how important it is for someone to really understand my pain point and challenges. I've made it my life's commitment to always help clients have a better program than they have ever had at their company.

*H*ERE, HOLD MY WINE MOMENT:
You may not always be the most popular person but at the end of the day, you have to do what you know is right. Be an advocate for your client. Or, in case you only interact with internal people, always do what is ethically right. People eventually will see your worth. So, stick out the hard stuff and be a leader in your own career. Make things happen.

Chapter 27: Adventures in Travel - Now the Funny Part Begins!!

Travel offers an opportunity to try new wine wherever you go!!

I've had so many people who say how cool it would be to travel for work. I understand the thought process, and for the most part, I've been very lucky to visit the places I have been able to visit: however, I have often found myself in all kinds of travel situations.

First of all, I have been lost in every city I have ever visited. I have had rental cars with flat tires, and planes that had near-misses in the air and on the ground. One time I was boarding a plane as the fire warning went off. As I was passing through the first-class cabin, this really cute guy looked at me and said, "Those pretty blue eyes just lit up on that one." I said back to him, "If this thing is going down, you better pass back those free drinks to me." We both laughed!

One time I had a guy sitting next to me who had to use the 'bag' to...well...you know what the bag is for, right?

Another time, a person was sick and sneezing all over everything. Then there was the guy who picked at his teeth the entire trip...nice! You still think that travel is glamorous?

Occasionally a nice person will help me with my luggage. For the most part, we 'road warriors,' as we are commonly called, have to fend for ourselves. And luggage is a lot heavier the wearier you become.

I had a coworker who also had terrible travel experiences. We both were tagged with the 'black cloud of travel' label. This coworker actually had one of the best stories. She hated using the restroom in an airplane, but this particular time she had no choice. She was trying to get up from the toilet and apparently, the toilet grabbed the bottom of her pants legs when she sat down. Her pants became so tight on her legs that she could not get up.

Trying to get out of the pants and trying everything she knew to get away from the attack toilet, she had to hit the 'call' button for a flight attendant to help her. Poor girl, it was the funniest thing I think I have ever heard happening while traveling.

I remember one of my very first implementations was with a client up on 'The Cape' in Massachusetts. I remember driving a long way but finally reaching the tiny hotel for the night. When entering my room, I realized the heat had not been turned on, and it was really cold. It took a long time for the heat to kick in, but I woke up in the middle of the night, and it was about 80 degrees in the room. Hotel rooms are not fun at all because it takes forever to get the room temperature right. By the time you get the temperature right, you have to leave!

I remember walking into my client meeting the next morning and with an apparent Southern accent to the people on the Cape, I smiled and said, "Good morning, how is everyone today?" The guy with whom I was meeting quickly said to me, "Stop with the Southern crap and tell me the ten things I need to do and get the hell out." I could feel my face turning bright red.

I wanted to say something to him, but when you are representing another company and its reputation, you have to be polite and keep your thoughts in check. I simply wiped the smile off of my face and handed him a document of the ten things he needed to do, asked if there were any additional questions, and then left.

*H*ERE, HOLD MY WINE MOMENT:
Traveling for work can present a world of challenges. Eating alone is something I am now used to, in addition to being lost everywhere you go. Remember that you need to be aware of your surroundings. Think before taking a job that requires a lot of travel and make sure you can handle being away from home most of the time. You need to also be very street-wise.

Section 3 – Ch-ch-ch-ch-ch-changes!

WE KNOW YOU ARE SINGING ALONG!
MILLENNIALS WHO ARE NOT SINGING -
HERE IS INFO ON DAVID BOWIE:
HTTPS://WWW.YOUTUBE.COM/WATCH?
V=XMQORYYO1YE

Chapter 28: Car - The Ole Girl

Like fine wine, this girl stuck around and only got better with age! Stay tuned, funny story on tap!

I HAD A 2003 PLYMOUTH LASER THAT MY FATHER HAD BOUGHT me brand new when I was struggling financially as a single mother. I kept that car for a very long time. She could turn on a dime when finding yard sale signs with my neighbor.

I had a great mechanic that kept the ole girl running. The best thing you can do for your car is to make sure the oil is changed on-time. I learned that from my mechanic father and my ex-husband.

Towards the 250,000-mile mark, I took the ole girl in for her regular blood transfusion (oil change in normal terms). My mechanic told me she was still a great car, but said, "Don't drive her long distances because everything on the car is wearing out!" He did not want me to get stuck anywhere.

Well, as you know by now, I travel for a living. Anytime I

had to travel from Virginia to Washington, D.C., I hated the horrible traffic. I would take the Amtrak train rather than trying to drive a rental car or even take my own car. If I had an appointment with clients and I drove, I would either be there early or very late depending on the traffic that day.

So, one day I had to go to a meeting in Maryland and was going to take the train again. I got to the train station and found out everything had been shut down due to some flooding waters. They had no prediction of when the trains would be working again.

I knew at that point if I was going to make my meeting, I had to drive. But I did not have time to get a rental car. So the ole girl was it that day. I decided since my mechanic had just changed her 'blood,' and she had her belts annually changed, that I would chance making my meeting on-time.

She was doing great, but then the traffic got heavier and heavier. There were trucks everywhere and I have to say, the ole girl was really scared. But I just talked her through it. We got to the meeting and everything was fine. Then we had to drive back home.

I got to the 495/95 interchange so I could get on 95 to get back to Richmond. Suddenly, she stopped. I made it to the side of the road, then what do you do? I called my AAA (auto club service) and was not guaranteed what time someone would get there, but they knew about my call and would keep in touch with me.

If any of you have ever been in that area, you know you cannot even walk off of the interstate because of fences (never mind the fact that I am wearing a business suit). It is amazing how even if you don't have to go to the bathroom, suddenly because you know you are stuck and cannot go, you have to go. You know what I mean? Lordy! It was also extremely hot that day.

Finally, a tow truck driver saw me and stopped. He said

he noticed a blonde in the car and wanted to see if I needed help. You see, sometimes it is good to be a blonde, right?

Thankfully, he was able to get her started. It was enough for me to follow him off the road until we could decide what I should do with her. Luckily, he was in the AAA network, and we decided to have him drive me back to Richmond with the ole girl on his flatbed truck. I think she was a little embarrassed. She didn't want to be viewed as a repo car that someone couldn't pay for. She didn't want to feel that cheap. And, she was upset she had let me down, but I knew she was going to be OK once we got her home.

So here I go climbing into the tow truck with my suit on heading to Richmond with a guy I did not know. Sometimes in life, you just gotta do what you gotta do and hope for the best. He was actually a very nice guy. He got me and the ole girl to a safe spot, and I was able to call a friend to pick me up and bring me home.

She didn't want me to leave her (she was a sensitive kind of girl you know). But she realized she was safe at the mechanic's shop with me leaving a note so her favorite mechanic (whom she thought was very handsome) would tend to her broken parts.

I've always been very dedicated to my job to make sure I get where I need to be on-time. I've been on flights with issues and have had to drive in many inches of snow to get to the airport only to be told the airport is shutting down. I once drove back in many inches of snow with a group of people from Philadelphia I didn't know because that airport was shut down.

The ole girl has since retired, but she was a great car. In all the years I had her, she only let me down that one time. Not a bad record, but maintenance is certainly key to keeping mechanical things going.

*H*ERE, HOLD MY WINE MOMENT:
Don't let excuses stop you from performing your job. Figure out a way and fulfill your duties. Bosses will laugh at your luck, but will appreciate your effort.

Chapter 29: Fiscal Responsibility and Different Culture

Let's be Franc here!

∼

I HAVE LEARNED TO KEEP AN OPEN MIND IN BUSINESS. I'VE ALSO learned about different cultures, different industries, and what makes them distinctive from the previous client. I learned quickly how to read people and know when I need to try to explain an idea or suggest another approach.

As in life, trust your instincts. Learn to laugh at the situations that happen to you and keep an open mind. Listen and learn. Sometimes, you will be surprised what you may learn.

Now that my career was progressing into a totally different direction than what I ever thought it would, I wanted to pause for a moment and tell you about something I learned during this time that really impacted me.

One event that impacted me was a loss in the financial industry with the passing of Ed Gilligan, President of American Express. And the other event was hearing a fabulous speaker, Frank Abagnale, whom I've heard three times at a conference (Institute of Financial Operations) I attended regularly. Frank is known as the "Catch Me If You Can" guy in the famous movie as portrayed by Leonardo DiCaprio.

Although neither of these men were or are personal friends of mine, the thought process for each man was amazing to me, in addition to how each of their thought processes correlated in my life as well. Let me explain.

Ed Gilligan touched many lives in his lifetime. He was a top executive at American Express. If you worked at Amex, you knew Ed. Amex is like a family. He did not see his 'job' as something he just did each day. The people he worked with were important to him. Early on, he found a mentor to help teach him about business. He chose someone in busi-ness he admired and wanted to emulate.

Once Ed started to become successful, he reached out to people he felt had his drive and ambition, and he helped by mentoring their careers. The only thing Ed asked was that they too would reach out and help others one day. Ed was the epitome of a great leader.

What I learned from Frank Abagnale was different but just as impactful. I learned when he spoke that the movie "Catch Me If You Can" was not a completely accurate depic-tion of Frank's life. I learned he was never even asked for his input for the content of the movie. After hearing Frank speak, I realized what a special man he really had become.

Frank talked a lot about his dad. He ran away from home at age sixteen. His parents never told him of a pending divorce, but instead a judge told him about it and said he had to decide who to live with at that very moment. Frank said he was blindsided by what the judge said to him. He loved both of his parents and found the decision to be impossible. So, he ran away, never to see his dad again.

At age fifty-five, his father had a freak accident and died. Frank learned months later about his father's death, which devastated him. He loved his father because he said each night, regardless of what time his father came home from work, he would creep into his children's bedrooms, kiss each one as they lay asleep, and tell them he loved them.

Frank stated to all of the men in the audience, "Anyone can be a father to a child, but it takes someone special to be a real daddy." He stressed that a real man does not cheat on his wife, and that a real man loves his wife and his children.

Frank also said that even though people have glamourized his life on the run as a criminal, he regrets every day the things he did to survive. He stated he still gets up in the middle of the night thinking that he could have been in prison camps overseas for the crimes he committed. And he is grateful for the U.S. Government for helping him come back home to the United States. Frank is still working for the FBI to fight crime and fraud today.

Frank gave great advice to all of us in the room. He stated, "Do not write checks unless you know the check is going directly to the financial institution. Think about it: you are handing the person your name, possibly your address, your full account number, and some people still have their phone and social security numbers on their checks." But obviously, the worst part is that you are handing over your full bank account number!

He also went on to say, "Do not use debit cards. Only use credit cards. If you have someone to charge something on your card, the credit card company will give you the money back as long as you let them know you have a fraudulent charge." Actually, after he shared that information, laws have changed. Now if a merchant accepts a card and does not verify the person using the card by checking their identification, or they use a Personal Identification Number or

PIN to verify the card, then the merchant will have to pay any fraudulent charges back to you. Check with your bank to see if their debit cards are now covered for any fraudulent activity. Some now are covered.

Being in the financial industry for a very long time, I have always said to eliminate checks both personally and in business. I've heard companies state that they would put mail to be picked up right outside of their office and a van would pull-up, take the mail out, redo the checks to 'lift' the payee and amount, and then the money would be stolen.

If you have ever heard of 'Positive Pay,' Frank actually invented that solution. The solution is a way for a business to send a file to the bank each day of the actual check numbers and amounts, payee name, and amount. If anything comes in differently, the bank will not honor that check.

HERE, HOLD MY WINE MOMENT:
Please consider each day of your life to make a difference in someone's life, including yours. Get a mentor. Be fiscally responsible and consider the suggestions that Frank and Ed have given throughout their careers.

Section 4 – Holidays

JINGLE BELLS, JINGLE BELLS, CABERNET ALL
THE WAY!

Chapter 30: Christmas and the Holidays

Ahhh, time for a nice time with family and get-togethers!

CHRISTMAS AND NEW YEAR HOLIDAYS ARE WONDERFUL memories for many of us. And, like so many of us, I have many memories of the past. I remember being that little girl growing up in a small town when everyone would dress up on Christmas Eve and visit each other before attending midnight mass. We would eat wonderful food and the adults would share a few spirits. I can remember a few of them falling asleep during the church service, too!

I also remember my dad picking me up in his arms and dancing to the joyous music. Christmas was always a glorious celebration of love and laughter. It was a wonderful celebration of family and friends gathering for hugs and presents.

I started thinking about the experiences I have had over my lifetime and thought I would share some stories that may remind you of some of your own holiday memories.

When I was a kid, I would bring out my hula-hoop and

stand for hours being the irritating kid in the middle of the room while the adults drank and ate. Mom would also send me in to hula-hoop when my brothers had dates visiting. I am sure my brothers were not happy about me being there either!

After the celebration, it was time to get ready for midnight mass. Church was the place where everyone we knew would come and would celebrate the birth of Christ. People attending were either relatives or great friends. It was always comforting to be surrounded by so many familiar faces.

I grew up with a lot of structure and certain beliefs. Then one day, I grew up and married a boy who stole my heart. We had a baby boy, and then right after the child was born, the husband left for someone new. Suddenly, holiday celebrations were very different.

After my husband left, times were very hard financially and emotionally. I can remember walking around the stores Christmas shopping with my hand on my son in the shopping cart in fear someone may snatch him away from me.

Each year I would save my pennies so we could go to a tree farm and cut a live Christmas tree. Yes, there were times when it was a cedar tree out in the woods because of money issues, but we always had fun picking out the perfect tree.

My in-laws each year would invite me to spend Christmas Eve with them. We would join the celebration, and enjoy opening gifts.

People ask me all the time about how I cope being alone during the holidays. So, I will tell you my theory about being alone during the 'joyous time of the year.' To me, any time of the year is joyous. I know it sounds cliché, but life is truly what you make it. I have a good life. I have accomplished a lot in my time on this earth. I never see my work as done.

So you would think unhappiness and depression would set in, right? Not in the least do I even think about being alone as something bad in my life. I actually clean up my kitchen, watch old movies, enjoy a nap, and really rest my mind.

You see, in my life I have filled it with so many friends and happy events that when it comes time when I am alone, I see it as a great thing. I love recharging my batteries, so to speak.

I volunteer with many things that give me a sense that I have done something to pay-forward. I have volunteered at the ALS Walk and gathered goods for the Veterans Hospital. I have had my 'swim' buddies over for a luncheon.

I give money to several organizations but one I am most proud of is helping organizations who help dogs from dog fighting rings and abused animals. Doing something for those who cannot help themselves is most rewarding.

So the next time you are worried about being alone, please do yourself a favor. Reflect on what you were able to do throughout the year to give back. How many friends did you talk through a crisis?

This year I gave a family heat when their furnace was not working. I have a fantastic heat and air guy, and he and his family are great friends of mine. He found a used unit and worked with me to help this family finally get heat in their home for Christmas.

When I end my year, I reflect and know that my love has reached many far and wide. And honestly, I am never alone. My heart is full with the reward of love received back from my good deeds.

I hope everyone has a very special Christmas and New Year. Let's bring the New Year in together and see what we both can get ourselves into to make the new year the best ever!

SPECIAL HAPPY HOUR MOMENT:

THE FUN PART OF DEALING WITH FAMILY DURING THE HOLIDAYS! OH MY!

During the Holidays, we get to deal with relatives and friends we may not have seen for at least a year. Some people we will be happy to see and others, not so much.

I was lucky because my ex-in-laws are awesome people. I was accepted as a daughter and sister. Our tradition in the Anderson household was also flanked with 'spirits' each year. One tradition was a family member who would always fall into the Christmas tree. We all looked forward to the familiar 'tradition' every year!

Neighbors would come as well, and there were familiar foods always prepared. We always looked forward to the turkey carefully placed into the oven to slow cook all night long. It was great to smell the turkey cooking as we ate and drank. What a fantastic memory.

Opening gifts was always fun. I can remember when I was divorced, I still was invited to the Anderson celebration. I had no money to buy gifts. Sometimes, the best thing was the $19.95 Olan Mills photography special during the holidays. I would scrape the money together and give pictures of my son as gifts. I think people knew I did not have a lot of money, but at the end of the day, it was the love we shared that was important.

I do believe Christmas has become too commercialized. As an adult now, I prefer to go out for a nice lunch or dinner with friends and family as opposed to buying gifts. And, many of my friends and family agree and we have so much more meaningful memories.

Money can be very hard for people and I really do believe there are other ways to spend time together and keep the gifts (in moderation) for the children who still believe. Well, as a matter of fact, I still believe so, if you want to get me a gift, feel free!

But, there are the relatives and/or friends who we know who are going to do what they can to embarrass us. Like the familiar sound ringing in my ears, "So, you are still single? Oh honey, the right guy will come along soon."

My mother moved in with me when I built my home. Our traditions changed once the 'home place' was sold and my Dad had passed. Mom and I would cook together and, along with my son, we would have a very quiet dinner for Christmas. We would spend Christmas Eve together opening our gifts.

I remember one year, Mom told me we had a relative living in the city whom we had not seen since she was a very young girl. We were invited to visit her and her husband (both lawyers) to spend the afternoon with them for the holiday.

So, in true tradition, my mother and I dressed up to go for the visit. My cousin's home was very elegant. We were offered wine and cookies. I had started a diet a few weeks before so I declined the cookies. My mother stated to my cousin, "Oh she struggles with her weight so, she will not eat the treats." Lovely!! Sometimes you just have to let it go. I chalked it up to Mom not really meaning it in a bad way.

My holidays today are lonely but happy. My mother passed away many years ago, so I cook a small dinner. My son will spend about an hour with me to eat. Usually, he is spending another meal with a girlfriend so my time is cut short.

I am OK with spending most of the time alone because I recharge my batteries so to speak. I can finally rest, regroup and get ready for the New Year!

So, here is my guide to surviving the traditional Christmas, keeping an open mind when blending families, and surviving the holiday alone.

- Understand that each person and family has their own idea of tradition.
- The holiday is about spending time with those you love and not pressing yourself to have to do certain things to make the holiday complete.
- Some are going to say something that may upset you.
- Remember, they are your relatives and, the day will end sooner than you think. Take a deep breath and relax.
- Keep the gifts to children only.
- If adults want to exchange gifts, make it very simple gifts, including a nice bottle of wine or something very simple and not too expensive.
- A meal together can be so powerful to spend time talking.
- Remember, not everyone has a lot of money to spend.
- Being alone can be good.
- Think about things that made you happy this year.

- Think about things when your judgement was not good.
- Make a plan to change the unhappy times in your life.
- If you're in a bad relationship, remember...it's not going to get better.
- Make a plan to break free and start fresh. You deserve to be happy.

When Christmas is coming, I will not see you in the store. I will be the one with a big smile on my face enjoying a nice lunch or dinner with people who are great friends and family. Keep it simple and, be thankful for all you have in your life. And if you are in a position to help someone in need, it will fill your heart with joy!

*H*ERE, HOLD MY WINE MOMENT:
It's human nature to want more than you have. Look around...you have all that you need.

Chapter 31: What Is Your Job Wish This Christmas? Ask Your Guardian Angel!

Wish upon a good Viognier!

With Christmas upon us, it's the time many of us wish for miracles to happen. But when we wish for something like a new job, it typically means it is not anything we can do for ourselves. A wish is a longing for something that we desire. Yet, at times, the wish can feel impossible to achieve. Or so we think.

I do believe when we really want something, we ourselves need to bring our dream to life. How in the world do we bring something to us we cannot control, you ask? Well, I really believe several things can help in your quest. Let me explain.

First, if something like a job is really meant to be, then it will eventually find its way. We just have to be open to accepting what we want and, depending what it is, we some-times need to put ourselves out there to actually let it happen and to be receptive to the dream coming to life.

Now, I do understand this step is hard. I have a hard time when it seems the dream will never happen or another person keeps telling you "NO." There have been times I feel like it's apparently not meant to be no matter how badly I want my wish to come true; however, you can never just give up your dream. The actual outcome may be telling you something better is on the way, and to be open to seeing the dream come true in a different form.

Think about a time when you knew you wanted that job. Rather than saying, "I will never get this job. I will interview, but if they hire me, I will be totally surprised." What do you think are the chances you will get the job if you go into the job thinking you are not good enough? Exactly. You got the idea now!

I have interviewed a lot of people in my business career. I have had people who looked like they were scared to death and if I had said 'boo,' I think they would have jumped out of their skin.

Instead, walk through the doors well groomed with a smile on your face. Greet the hiring manager with a warm and likable personality, and a medium firm handshake. Look the interviewer in the eyes. Listen to the questions carefully and answer honestly and thoughtfully.

When I have someone interviewing with me, I try to make them feel at ease. Employers want to see the real you. Think about it, if you have someone in front of you who is straight faced, does not look you in the eye and looks frightened, then chances are, the person who walks in, head held high, smiling and personable will appear more confident than the frightened candidate. Be someone who that person can see working with and enjoying being around. I bet you will be a front-runner if you do the things I mentioned!

Second, if I really want something, I will close my eyes and imagine how it will be to have my dreams come true. I know that may sound a little strange, but sometimes, we need to envision what we want actually happening to us in our minds before it will happen. We need to understand how good it will feel to finally receive that job we want, or the house we pray for, or the love you have always wanted in your life. Anything can happen if you bring a strong belief when thinking about your wish and how your life will transform when your wish is finally fulfilled.

I feel strongly that people will get what they want with positive energy around them. We have to create that energy ourselves.

To create a positive energy, be kind. Nothing will ever work in your life if you always have a horrible attitude. If you have a grim look on your face and appear as an unapproachable kind of person, not much is going to come your way. And I know a few people with horrible attitudes. I stay clear of those grumpy people! Think about it: would you rather be around a happy person or someone who is going to complain the whole time you are around them? I really believe those people haven't a clue how awful they are to be around. Honestly, I don't know how someone cannot know how mean they are acting. But for some people, they don't seem to care how rude they can be. After all, their life is horrible. And I can certainly see why.

Instead, just be kind to people as they walk by, and smile. Pull in the right people with an approachable style. Look people in the eye and be honest above all else. People like to know they can count on someone. Also, be fun. People want to be around people who know how to laugh and enjoy life. I have life-long friends who I may not see for months or years at a time, but I know at any time either of us really needs support or need each other, we get together and we have not skipped a beat in our friendship.

Think now about something you really want. Got it in your mind? Now take time when it is quiet and close your eyes and think about how your life would be when your wish comes true. Notice I said, 'when' your wish comes true? You ever heard of daydreams? Daydream a little and the feeling will be fantastic. Sometimes, I have had a daydream and when it actually happens in real life, it is almost spooky when you know the events that will occur before they happen. This is the time that you start thinking and strange music goes off in your head like a scary movie, right?

You have a guardian angel just like I do. I know my guardian angel is my father. Ever since my dad passed away, I have always felt he has guided me through life, and you can probably tell I have made some fantastic wishes come true. As a matter of fact, I have been pretty successful in my career, and as far as my life goes, I have been able to design a home when I had no money and eventually, I had it built.

I have been able to go from a filing clerk to working for some of the largest companies in the world. And it is not because I am smarter than anyone else, or have something nobody else possesses. It's because people enjoy being around me and they trust me. They know I will make sure a job gets done. I am honest about what I do not know, and I surround myself with fantastic people who can help me with what I lack in abilities. And, I take the opportunity to learn from them and help them with their shortcomings too!

*H*ERE, HOLD MY WINE MOMENT:

Sometimes you need to believe in yourself to draw what you want to come to you. And, sometimes it's 'magic' you let into your life. Either way, if you keep a positive outlook, even when things get hard, you will be successful. You will be happy. Trust yourself with the wish by enabling positive thoughts. Trust in the magic of the Christmas spirit to help bring you that job wish you want to make a reality. Believe in yourself and you can make any path you want in life come true.

Chapter 32: When the New Year Comes!

Champagne (France); Cava (Spain); Prosecco (Italy); Sparkling – Everything in-between!!

WITH THE NEW YEAR'S CELEBRATIONS, I ALWAYS FEEL VERY optimistic! I have a job that I love, wonderful family and friends, and I am lucky to have loving furry babies who bring a ton of joy to my everyday life. And you know what? I created my life and made it happy to live each and every day.

People ask me all of the time why I am so happy. My happiness was a journey, a well-planned journey. So, how can you make a plan starting today? Let's explore Robin's guide to a happy life.

The key to happiness first is to love yourself. Sounds easy, right? It's the hardest part of this journey you will take. We all have things we do not like about ourselves: our weight, our name, our money situation, our hair, our height, and on and on.

How do you tackle learning how to love yourself? First

of all, you need to figure out what you can change (and remember, you have to want to change).

The big obstacle I tackled was stress. All of us have a certain amount of it, so we all need to learn how to cope with stress. Stress is probably one of the most dangerous things to our wellbeing.

Even if there was a tragedy or a lot of sorrow in your life, you can change the way you react to certain events. When my parents died, at first it seemed hard to learn to live without them; however, I thought about the life they were able to lead. I knew they were now happy to be out of pain. So I chose to concentrate about how lucky I was to have great parents and how happy they were now to see relatives and great friends who had passed. I am very certain my mother is the director of fun things to do up there!

By looking at death in a different way, the grief was lessened and helped me to become the strong woman I am today. I live life to the fullest every single day. I find something good in every day.

When a child is screaming, is it because they truly have hurt themselves, or is it because they are not getting their way? I've been around many young mothers who are dealing with an unruly child.

I remember once time when I had to go to Hawaii on business (hard job, right?). My coworker and I booked a Hawaiian luau. It's a food feast where they cook the pig in the ground and have all kinds of food in a buffet-like setting. We were seated next to a couple that had a little boy. The little boy was screaming at the top of his lungs and the parents could not control him.

I asked the young parents if I could take him to go get them another drink. They were desperate so they let me pick him up. He and I went to the drink station. I told him that his daddy wanted a drink and I wanted him to decide what his dad would have. So when we went up to the station, he took his time and heard all of the options and then he decided what his Dad would like to drink. He was so proud he was able to be such an important 'big' boy in making such a fun decision. The little boy felt important, and after that, his parents learned a very valuable skill.

Kids need direction and, sometimes they just want to feel important too. I've been in many homes with children. I walk in and see nothing on the tables within reach of a child. I never took anything down in my home. I taught my son what was right and what was wrong. I could take him anywhere and he knew when I said 'no' that he could not touch certain things. He listened. I think sometimes we let stressful situations rule us and we add obstacles that can make it worse rather than dealing with things head-on.

If you have a boss who is really mean and hateful, what do you do? When there is a workplace situation causing me pain, I take action right away. I usually sit down with the person and talk things through. A lot of times, people are upset about other things in their lives and have no idea how they are coming across in business.

Or perhaps you are doing something that the boss has not talked to you about. It may be something you can change but the boss has not told you. You will have an opportunity to learn what you can possibly do to make the situation better for both of you. Always communicate rather than harbor bad feelings.

You have to decide what makes YOU happy, not someone else. I know so many people who 'live' for other people. Just my humble opinion, but, if you want to be truly happy, 'live' for yourself. Beyond kids, beyond the spouse, make time for you and something you want to do! If you do not take the time to work on you, nobody else will.

So, take the time and come up with a 'happy' plan.

When you do have a significant other, you do want to consider what makes them happy as well. And hopefully, you have chosen a partner who enjoys the same things as you do. If not, please do not stay in a bad situation. Find a way to get out- life is way too short.

It is amazing to me how many people will approach me and tell me what a nice smile I have. Generally speaking, people want to be around people who are happy.

Friends are especially important to my circle of happiness. If someone disrespects me, I do not try to change them or their belief to my way of thinking. I simply will move on with other friends who are happy. I do not expend energy on unhappy people. The unhappy is not where I spend my positive energy.

So, what are some things I do to help me in my life's journey?

Sleep – Sleep is so important to overall health. I know we all have sleepless nights from time to time. It's normal to take the weight of the world on your shoulders; however, if you can help control your stress, you will feel so much more relaxed at night.

Take a brisk walk to clear your head. Make sure you are physically tired. Take a hot bath and then go to bed and turn the TV off! Relax and sleep. Leave the worry behind. Worry only hurts you and solves nothing.

Take care of yourself – Figure out a form of exercise you enjoy. Do not join a gym and do things you do not like. If you enjoy running, form a group and hold each other accountable. Meet new people who enjoy your passion too. Meeting new people is a great way to improve your happi-ness with expanding your circle of friends.

Friends – I have enjoyed the people I have met and have also become my friends. Making new friendships is very important to your mental wellbeing. It's nice to have people who care about you and it is a fantastic feeling.

Eat well – I know we all have that one or two or three things we love so much. I love ice cream and chocolate. I do not deprive myself; however, I make goals for myself. Once I reach a goal, I will reward myself with a treat that I love. Remember if you start a diet and think you can never enjoy that bowl of ice cream or special cookie, then you are looking at diet in the wrong way.

Make a goal (for example) to lose ten pounds within four or five weeks. Then pick a special day and know you can enjoy a treat at the end of that journey. Then set another goal. Maybe the next ten pounds you do the same. Remember that one to two pounds per week in weight loss is a healthier way than crash diets of ten pounds a week. You will not keep the weight off and will pack on more in the end because you will be depriving your body what you need to stay healthy.

Exercise your mind – Learn something new. Try something new. Keep your mind working all the time. Read a good book. Even if you only have ten minutes to read before bed, do something for you. And, make it a fun book, not a 'self-help' book. I feel those books just make you worry more, especially if you cannot make the changes you need; then you will feel defeated.

Robin's great tips to remember:

- The past cannot be changed – move on – strong people don't waste time feeling sorry for themselves.
- Embrace change – it's going to happen, so be a part of the change and have a say.
- Take a calculated risk – you will have nothing in life if you do not take risks.

- Celebrate other people's success and remember to always celebrate yours.
- Opinions do not define your reality.
- Everyone's journey is different.
- Everything gets better with time – give it time to work through.
- Judgments are a confession of character.
- Overthinking will lead to sadness.
- Happiness is found within – do not depend on someone else to make you happy, and do not expend energy on things you cannot control.
- Positive thoughts create positive things to happen.
- Smiles are contagious – except for the very unhappy person – leave the 'grumpy butts' to their own misery.
- Kindness is free.
- You only fail if you quit – never quit.
- Some people will never change – stop trying to change them.
- What goes around, comes around.
- Rejection is good; it just means you are being redirected to something much better.

If you want this to be 'your' year, do not just sit on the couch and wait. Be kind to you! Go out and make a change. Smile more. Be excited. Do new things. Meet new people. Get rid of the clutter in your life. Stay away from negative people or people who are, as I call them, a train wreck Harry. These are the kind of people who are always draining you emotionally, and they believe nothing you do is right. Leave those people alone. There is no need for negativity when you have your 'happy' plan in full force.

Go to bed early and wake up early, refreshed, and ready

to take on a new day. Show more gratitude. Respect others at all costs. Do things that challenge you out of your comfort zone. Most of all, be brave...you can control your future.

*H*ERE, HOLD MY WINE MOMENT:
Take care of you first. If you are not in a good place mentally and physically, you will not be any help to others. It is a great time for that fresh start. Let's both smile right now and change the negative from last year and make the upcoming year the best year of our lives!

Chapter 33: Valentine's Day

You ever thought, "Life is like a box of chocolates?" Try Noche...it is a chocolate wine blend from a local winery very close to my home.

IN 2010, A FRIEND AND I VISITED ABBADIA ARDENGA Vineyard for a Brunello tour in Montalcino, Italy. Mario was a very old vineyard owner and winemaker. He asked where we were from. When the interpreter told him we were from Virginia, he stated, "Ah, Virginia is for Lovers!"

When it's Valentine's Day, you can hear heartbreak at every turn. People are either going out to dating sites, gyms, or bars, etc., to try and finally meet that 'perfect' person. Or they are going back to someone because 'it's better than being alone.'

The month of love really does not need to be a depressing time in your life. I have met so many people who feel they have to find someone in their life to be happy. I have heard the saying, "I need someone to 'complete' me."

Never, ever look for someone else to complete you. It is

your job to make sure you embrace who you are and be happy. Only when you are happy with you is when you find someone worthy to share your life.

Loving yourself gives you the strength to not put your happiness on someone else's shoulders. When you force someone to love you, I have to ask...how is that working out for you? I know so many people who get married just for the sake of not being alone. It seems the thought of being alone is such a fearful situation.

Years ago a family member who married for the third time came to visit me and my husband. His new wife seemed to be very nice. That evening, I fixed dinner. We all stayed in and had a few drinks. When his new wife turned into a very sloppy drunk, he looked at us and said, "It's amazing what you will do to keep from being alone." I have never forgotten his words and the look on his face when he realized he was not happy. The situation was so sad. I could see the sadness in his eyes.

Now do not get me wrong, finding the 'right' person is great. I hope one day I will too. However, so many people settle for what is not right for them just so they will not be alone.

People tend to think if they change themselves enough to 'make' the person love them, all will be perfect. Trust me; you will lose respect of the other person, guaranteed! This type of thought process can make for a very sad and unhappy situation.

I've seen the couples who are openly fighting in public. A lot of times settling is the reason people do not end up with the right person. The motivation for the union is driven by something else. Sometimes it's financial help or loneliness. Tell the truth, have you tried to buy someone's love? I thought so!

Loneliness is like a drug. A person will do anything to

keep from being lonely. If you can't stand to be alone, then why do you think anyone wants to be alone with you? Or, there's the heartbreak of the abuser whose spouse keeps coming back because they feel they have the power to change and save them.

Love is a very strong emotion; however, do not let the emotion rule you or change who you really are. Instead, find the right person. A person who really wants to be with you is a good start. If a person walks away, do not run after them. There is a reason they walked away. Let it go!

(Wasn't that a song? Ah, I can hear you singing it now.)

I look at couples who are perfect for each other, and it is a wonderful sight to behold. When I look at couples who truly are in love and their marriage is very strong (I like to use strong rather than perfect because I believe the word perfect is not easy to maintain), there are certain traits the couple has between them.

1. They are totally committed to each other and their marriage.
2. They talk about their spouse/partner to others in a loving way.
3. They do things together.

I remember going on a cruise. My friend and I were paired up with a very sophisticated couple for dinner. The two were always dressed so elegantly. They spoke about the bed they had, which were two bunk beds not to their liking. So, they took the mattress off and made one bed on the floor so they could be together. Oh, how romantic!!

She would take a sip of the soup, he would patiently wait for her thoughts and as soon as she said she liked the soup, he would then take a taste. He would state she was right and how he liked the soup as well. I had never seen anything quite like this couple.

Now not everyone has to be this gushy about how they are to each other; however, you could tell this couple respected each other so much and made each day together count. We later found out he was a Brigadier General.

He did not want us to know his status because the couple just wanted to enjoy everyone they met without everyone knowing his superior military status. They even ordered us some kind of cordial that had anisette in it. It had coffee beans too but tasted like licorice.

It was awful but we choked it down because we did not want them to think we were the two country bumpkins that we really were. It was a funny but eye-opening experience watching this lovely couple!

As a single person, what are our steps to finding love, the right kind of love and happiness?

Take steps to first decide who you are and what makes you happy.

1. Friends – they are important. Touch base with old friends, and make new friends.
2. Remember, you do not need a lot of friends, just the right friends.
3. Friends have friends who are possibly single.
4. Try different activities – if you do not like one you tried, try another.
5. If you meet someone who has the same interests, then that is a big step.
6. Learn to not take things so personally.
7. What other people think about you is none of your business.
8. Stay strong and believe in who you are...and, that is FANTASTIC!

9. Be happy – Put a smile on that face! Nobody wants to be with a Debbie downer.

I cannot tell you how many times people have been attracted to my smile. I was in the gym the other day and when I walked in, a man who comes for a pool workout said to me, "Robin, I just have to ask, do you always smile?"

I explained, "Why yes I do, I wake up smiling because I am happy." And then he finished with saying, "You make a bad day turn happy and bright, and I want to thank you for always bringing joy to our water group."

*H*ERE, HOLD MY WINE MOMENT:
The most important thing you can do in your life is to simply be happy. So start working today on your 'happy' and start enjoying life and attracting the right people to your life. Just think, we both may have a very nice Valentine's date next year. I will be the one with the big smile on my face. (Hopefully!)

Chapter 34: Mother's Day - Entitled Children

A mother needs her 'Momma' juice every now and then to deal with the kids!

~

MAY IS WHEN WE HONOR OUR MOTHERS. IT ALWAYS MAKES ME think about how I was raised versus how people handle their children today.

When I was very young, we were taught that when we reached twenty-one years old, we needed to be out of the house and on our own. And I followed my parents' rules. After that certain age, I was responsible for paying my own bills and no longer received assistance from my parents. However, today there are so many children who still receive assistance from their parents. Many kids expect their parents to pay for everything from their cell phone to car insurance, and sometimes even their rent or house payment.

I recently met a lady while at my doctor's office. She looked upset, so I started a conversation with her to see if I could help her relax. She suddenly started pouring her heart out to me about her son who had moved back in with her and her husband. Her son had access to her bank debit card. He did not pay rent nor did he bring food into the home. She also told me her son recently boasted about winning $1,000.00 in a contest and how hurt she was that he did not even consider helping her out with bills.

I asked her if her son had a job, and she responded he did. She stated his money went for special clothing and going out with friends all the time. This woman continued to explain she wanted to retire but could not because of the burden she had with her twenty-seven-year-old son. I could not help but think she was not alone with what had happened in her life with her child. At what point do we as parent have to continue the 'life support' to our children? Well, typically, eighteen is the end of the 'legal' obligation.

The only reason I know this legal fact was because of advice I received from my lawyer when I was getting a divorce. My lawyer explained the age limitation to me when I wanted to include education as a part of child support. Of course, each state can have different laws, so please get legal advice from someone who is qualified to guide you on matters of legal responsibility with children.

I firmly believe if there is a way to have our children educated, I am all for saving for their future as long as you have the means to pay for the savings account.

Besides education, I have noticed our society today has made our children's lives more important than our own lives sometimes. I know I have put my child first many times to 'help,' when in actuality I was hurting both him and my financial well-being! And it took a complete stranger explaining to me that my constant support to ensure everything was perfect with my son's life was not preparing him for the future without me one day.

I had never thought about the fact that I was doing more

harm than good by always being there and never letting my child fall.

I am certain there are many of us reading this right now who, admittedly or not, have done the same as I have at some point. And one day, any of us could be in a hard financial position of supporting adult children just like the lady I met. I think a good 'wake-up' call and a good 'shaking' needs to happen to anyone who has fallen into the 'loving too much' trap. And believe me, it happens before you even realize it!

I have heard many people say most kids of the current generation feel they are entitled to their parents' help taking care of their every need.

So, when do we stop helping our adult kids? I think it is really hard to set a certain timeframe due to many different circumstances. So you have to be the judge of your own children, and where they are in their life at any point.

Below are a few guidelines that may help us all gauge steps to take to break free quicker!

1. **Start early teaching your children to have real responsibility.**

Even young children should learn to take care of their own things, but make sure material things are kept to a minimum.

Each day, make sure your children pick up toys, make their bed, etc. Make them feel important by letting them help decide a meal and help cook.

2. **Teach your children respect for others.**

When given gifts, have your children write thank-you notes. This is an age-old art that is so important, but we are losing sight of this wonderful gesture of appreciation.

Make it a fun activity by going to the mailbox or post office together.

Do not 'put up' everything in your house to keep the

child from being hurt. Teach them the word 'NO.' You need to have nice things in your home you enjoy.

When you do say 'NO,' make sure you do not cave in and give something to the child because you want them to stop whining. Have them raise money for a good cause (and they will feel so proud).

3. For older children who want something, make them work for it.

In today's world of cell phones and cars and fancy clothes, buy within reason.

If your child is younger, have them do chores around the house to earn money.

If older, have them get a babysitting job, cutting grass, etc.

If children are of working age, grocery stores or fast food restaurant positionsare usually easy jobs to get started. If they want those special pair of jeans, let them work and pay for them.

4. Find a cause in which your child may be interested in working.

There is so much we all can learn from our elders. Have your children learn to appreciate the older adults early on.

If a family in your community has lost their house to a fire or lost a loved one, show your child compassion for others.

Volunteering at a hospital, daycare, homeless or animal shelter is always eye opening.

The sooner children learn respect, empathy, compassion and responsibility, the easier their life will be and yours as well.

The road as a parent is hard. And as mothers, we all tend to want to help our children with everything and make life 'easier for them than it was for us.'

Instill in your children the lessons of life while you are there to help them if they fall. Your responsibility as a parent is to teach your children, not to take care of them as they become an adult!

To protect your young is absolutely your job, but when of an adult age, make sure you have a timeframe plan to transition them into their own life.

*H*ERE, HOLD MY WINE MOMENT:
On Mother's Day, please, let your children do something nice for you on your very special day! Ask for a new high-tech cell phone!!

Section 5 - Written with a Lot of Love and Plenty of Wine

HECK WITH A GLASS...THIS NEEDS A WHOLE BOTTLE!

Note: May want to steer clear unless you know you can handle this!

Chapter 35: How to Write the 'Death Email'

Italy was the first place I ever had grappa. I'm not a fan of grappa! Grappa is a liquor made with cedro, which is an Italian fruit similar to an oversized lemon. Anyway, I am not a fan, but you are welcome to try it!

∾

A WHILE BACK, I MET A GUY WHO WAS A LITTLE OLDER THAN me. For me, that is a bit unusual because I usually date men who are either younger or about my age. I was not attracted to this guy, but it had been a good while since I had dated, and my friends told me to keep an open mind.

So for the first date, he had me meet him for an outdoor concert. The concert was fun. I can tell you that his dancing was horrific and very embarrassing! He had the arms flinging around, his feet were off-balance, and he was shuffling with his head bobbing back and forth. I figured, you got to give him credit for enjoying himself.

I went out with him a few more times. Whenever we went out to eat, I always had to 'share' his plate of food. I was only able to get my own food when other couples were around and everyone was 'allowed' to get their own plate.

Once, when he was not hungry, I had not eaten all day and wanted to get something before I had a glass of wine. I was allowed food then, and of course, he had to have a bite, but I was okay with him eating when drinking.

Another time was when we were with a group of his friends, we went to a restaurant and he 'allowed' me to get my own plate. During that time, one of the girls in the group came up to me and said, "He is a really nice guy, very giving. He can just be persnickety sometimes." OK, that comment was put in the databanks. It's amazing what you can learn from their friends.

One day when we went to another outdoor concert, a couple he knew met us there. The woman said to me, "He is really taken by you." So, I asked, "Oh, so what has he told you about me?" And she said, "He is very impressed how successful you are and the nice home you have." She went on to say to me, "But, he can be very controlling." Another little tidbit for the databanks, wouldn't you say?

I looked at her and said, "Oh, he won't control me." And she said, "Good for you."

For our next date, he wanted to take me to a really great barbeque place. We walked in and he was all excited like a kid in a candy store. He said, "I'm going to get the sampler platter with chicken BBQ and ribs. What do you want?" And, I said, "I will also get a sampler platter." I started naming my items I wanted and he immediately stopped me and said, "We are getting one plate. Do you want cornbread or a biscuit?" I just said, "Whatever you want." And I said it pretty sarcastically, but either he ignored it or did not hear me saying it in a 'special' way.

There were other red flags. He had invited me to come to his ocean-front beach house – actually it was a timeshare, but he made it sound MUCH better than it was. He had several people coming that weekend. He explained to me that the water was not good there, so I brought two cases of bottled water when I was only going to be there for two days.

I do drink a lot of water, so wanted to be sure I was not imposing. I went to grab a bottle of water out of the refrigerator and he yelled at me and told me that water was for the beach and to get a glass out of the cabinet and use the filtered water out of the refrigerator. Really? I could not believe myself, but remembered my friends telling me in the back of my head to give this ugly man a chance.

I had also brought a lot of food items, plus a lot of wine and was going to do a wine pairing with each of the wines I brought with me. So, I certainly felt I had contributed to the cause and if I wanted a bottled water, I should have been allowed to get one without fighting about it!

His friends also wanted to go play putt-putt and go to a restaurant, and he was not happy. He stopped the putt-putt outing, but finally agreed to the restaurant outing as long as HE picked the place to go.

I also explained to him when I got there that I had not seen that beach since I was a young girl when my parents would go there all the time and that I would love to see how it changed. He ignored me. After watching how he interacted with people, I realized he apparently felt he paid so much to have his timeshare weeks that he wanted everyone to be there with him 24/7 during his time he had there.

He also would drive like a bat out of you know where. I think he enjoyed scaring me. He would almost run over his dog and when I would show concern for the dog, he yelled at me to STOP.

I had to go out of town one Tuesday for work and was going to have to get up early to go to the airport. He begged me to see him before I left and wanted to bring out his dog to meet my dog to see if they would get along. I said okay, but I could not make it a long night. I cooked dinner so he could bring his dog out to meet my dog.

Well, he walks through the door with an appetizer he had left over from having lunch with his daughter that day. I had a bottle of red wine opened for dinner, but he demanded this appetizer needed a white. So, I opened a bottle of white and we ate the appetizer (honestly, it was awful) and drank the bottle of wine.

Afterwards, I served dinner and we drank that bottle of wine also. Although we had two bottles of wine, we ate a lot of food, so I was not feeling tipsy at all, but apparently, he was...or at least I hope that is what it was...

After dinner, he sat down on the couch and started watching TV. While I was cleaning up the dishes, he was commenting on a show he was watching that I had never seen before. When I finished the dishes, I sat down on the couch while we were still talking about the show. He then told me to come sit by him. As soon as I sat by him, he threw his arm around me and started to try to grope me. I grabbed his hand and asked him what he thought he was doing. He then said, "I think you need to take your shirt off." And, I said, "Are you out of your mind? Is that all you came here for?" And he said, "Well, I thought since you were going out-of-town that you wanted to 'get lucky' before you left."

Guys, if you are doing this to a girl, please at least start with some romance. How in the world do you go from talking about a comedy TV show to groping someone? I'd say a lot over the top if you ask me!!

Needless to say, I was furious and said, "I don't know who you think you are to act this way, but it is time for you to go." So he said, "So, I'm not spending the night?" And, I said, "Absolutely not, I told you I had an early

180

flight in the morning, and I have a lot to do to get ready before my flight leaves."

He then stated, "Well, then you are going to have to get me crackers or something to eat because I cannot drive like this."

I immediately got up, went into the pantry and grabbed some crackers and asked him, "Do you want cheese too?"

So, he and his little dog left. I should have known when his little dog attack and drew blood on my pit bull, who is as sweet as they come, and my baby did nothing to his dog. I guess his dog is hateful just like he is.

And, I actually love dogs, so there you go!

After he left, my sleep was messed up because I was angry about the situation. I got up extra early and wrote him the 'death' e-mail. In a nutshell, I told him I did not appreciate the way he acted and there were red flags about the relationship that I did not like.

I stuck to the facts when I was writing it. I was angry when I wrote it, so I had to reread it before I sent it. Here are my tips for writing a good 'death' e-mail.

1. Think of all the things that you know you like about the person and do write some good things. After all, you would not have started dating the person if you didn't like something about them.
2. Do thank them for the nice things they did for you.
3. Stick with facts of things that happened that you do not like and explain why you do not like them.
4. Stick to your guns when you explain why you feel the relationship would fail.
5. Admit there may have been things the other person may not have like about you and owe those items. At this point, you may not hear what

that person thought, but that is OK. Nobody is perfect.

6. Wish them well and that you hope they will one day find the right person.

7. Then leave it alone.

I was grateful I never heard from him and felt very relieved I did not have to deal with his strange behavior anymore.

*H*ERE, HOLD MY WINE MOMENT:
Be true to who you are. If a red flag goes up, notice it and get out while you can!

Chapter 36: Go Ahead...Make Someone's Day!

Hey, hey, Chardonnay!/Let's make someone's day today! (That's the cheerleader coming out in me!)

EACH DAY I SET OUT TO MAKE A DIFFERENCE IN SOMEONE'S life.

I recently went grocery shopping and a very nice lady working in the produce section was getting ready to put out some fresh lemons. We started talking and I could tell she was going through a pretty rough time in her life. I decided she just needed to talk to someone and know that time would get better. I encouraged her without ever really knowing what was troubling her and when we finished, she hugged me and said, "You are exactly what I needed today."

We have to be there for people today. There are so many people who have things going on that we may never understand, but it is very important to them. Just being there to lend an encouraging word for her made all the difference in the world.

I have run across people who are caregivers for a loved one and can see in their face how much pain they are going through. I think a lot of us who have never been a caregiver before can't even imagine the heartache these family members go through to care for their loved one. Then when the loved one is gone, there is a sense of guilt that they have, thinking they could have done more.

I try to encourage people because I had a very different kind of heartache, and my belief may be a little over the top for some people, but it is what I believe. I was lucky that I was with both of my parents when their time came to pass to another life. I do believe when we die, we do go on to some-thing much greater than we are living here.

As I mentioned, I know that my father is my guardian angel. He had several brain tumor operations over the course of more than twenty years. His tumor was not malignant, but because the tumor was wrapped around the brain stem, they could never totally remove the growth. So every few years, it would grow back to where it affected his ability to do normal activities and he had to be operated on again.

One day, after all he had been through, his heart started to give out. The doctor came to the family and told us his kidneys were shutting down. He said if we wanted to keep him going, we would have to put him on dialysis, but his quality of life would not be as good as it was before he was sick the last time. My dad had started to falter a lot in the later years and we knew it would be hard for him in his aging years to fight anymore. So we decided to let him go.

The family surrounded him as he took his last breath and said a prayer. My mother ended with a Catholic prayer by herself. When someone passes, they expel the final breath and when he did, he sounded like a horse.

It was a strange moment for all of us because on one

hand, you realize he has passed on to his new life. On the other hand...well, you gotta know me to understand why I do this, but I said, "Daddy always did have to have the last word." And the whole family laughed.

It was a special moment, and I know my dad would have wanted us to know he was now out of pain and we were to rejoice that he was now on to his next life.

At my dad's funeral, I was smiling as I met people in line who were offering their condolences. People were asking me why I was smiling and I said he was happy and had no more pain. And, I was happy for him. I did not know why I had a sense of peace, but I did.

When my mother passed, it was a little more shocking, although she was eighty-eight years old when she passed. She got up that morning and ate her cinnamon bun and drank her coffee like she always did.

We were heading to the grocery store as we normally did. As soon as we were on the interstate, she grabbed her back, said it was hurting and that she was in severe pain. I thought maybe she had pulled her back out and decided that we were going to go directly to the doctor.

Of course, true to how my mother reacted, she did not want to go to the doctor, but all of a sudden, she stopped breathing as I was driving. I had several miles to go to the next exit and called 911. I was beating her on the chest with one hand while I drove with my knee and talked to the 911 operator.

I managed to get her breathing but she did not wake up yet. When I got to the exit, I pulled her out of the car. Luckily, two off duty medical people stopped to help me. They did not have any equipment, but they did manage to get her awake and were talking to her, although she was very confused.

Long story short, when she was at the hospital, she seemed okay until after a CAT scan. Then she was not breathing again. I had told them she had a 'Do Not Resuscitate Order,' but they started to do compressions and breathing anyway.

The doctor told me and my brother that her heart was still beating but not enough to sustain her, so we said to let her go. Luckily most of our family was with her when she passed. Again, we were able to pray while holding hands as she slipped away.

That night, as you can imagine, I had a hard time sleeping. I had the guilt of wondering if I could have done anything different or if I should have revived her in the car. We found out that she died of an aortic aneurysm, which is extremely painful. Then I felt very guilty that I brought her back to feel so much more pain.

But in the time I was trying to sleep, my mother appeared to me. She obviously wanted to get a message to me, and boy, did she ever. She was very young looking and had a big smile on her face. She was very excited and told me she ran into a lot of relatives and friends. She was naming them off one by one. I would have never remembered or could have made up all of those names so I know it was real.

She told me that the next day she was going to see another set of friends and family. Then she went away. But I do know she is with me still to visit because I smell her perfume every now and then in my home where she lived with me.

So when I meet someone who is grieving for someone, I tell them my mother is up there. She is like the cruise director of activities and she is in charge of showing their loved ones the ropes!! If nothing else, I get a smile out of them. Hopefully I give them some sense of comfort that their loved one is very happy, has chosen younger body, and is meeting all of their friends and relatives up there!!

I do believe there is happiness where people pass away. There is no more pain, and they are glad to be back with those they love who have passed on as well.

We need the responsibility when we meet someone to help them in their time of grief. Sometimes it can be almost impossible to bear, but we need to let them know their loved one is doing great and one day, we will meet them again.

*H*ERE, HOLD MY WINE MOMENT:
So for today and tomorrow, think about making someone's day at work or even in the grocery store. Pay someone's toll behind you, or just give someone a smile. Reach out to someone at work who you know is struggling in some way. Help that person to laugh at something or make them feel appreciated.

Chapter 37: It's All About the Nate...No Other Doggies!

Chateau Morrissette Old Dog Blue Wine...Nate is my Old Dog Blue!

～

I grew up with dogs and cats. My grandparents had Bobtail cats and Persians, so I learned a love of a pet early on in my life.

I mostly had dogs as I got older. I think I related to dogs more simply because when I wanted a dog to come to me they would, and a cat, well...you know how most of them can be, but I love cats and any other animal as well. Except for snakes and spiders. Not my favorite.

When I was married, we got a family breed dog we named Daniel's Irish Whiskey, an Irish Setter. I really loved Whiskey, as we called him. Unfortunately, Whiskey had a gastric torsion and had to have emergency surgery. The vet had to cut him open to flip his stomach back over. I was so upset. I had to go back to work the next day because it was closing and nobody could do my work.

He hung in there for a while, but ten days after his

surgery, he died. Whiskey's death was very hard on me. I tried so hard to save him, but couldn't. I was with him when he died. I don't think I have ever cried that much in my life. The love of a dog is such a strong bond.

I also got a dog when a guy I was dating took my son with him one day and went to the SPCA. He brought him by my work and asked me for $50.00 to adopt the dog. He was a very cute blonde lab we named Fred. I can't go to a shelter or SPCA because I will either dream about all of the pets for months or I would want to bring all of them home. It hurts my heart to go to those places.

Fred was such a good dog. Sometimes I think when you rescue a pet, they appreciate their home more because they know you saved them.

Fred was beautiful, jumping from rock to rock along the James River in Richmond. He was extremely smart. As he grew older, I thought he had hurt his leg, but it was actually his back. It about killed us all, but we eventually had to put Fred down when his mind was still good, but his back was hurting so bad he would yelp day and night. I could not let him be in that kind of pain.

My son rescued my current dog, Nate. The girl my son was seeing at the time had a brother who called my son and said, "You need to help me rescue this dog." Long story short, this beautiful pit bull puppy had been left in a crate for four or five days along with no food or water. These boys rescued him and took him to the vet. The vet stated if he had been left another forty-five minutes, he would probably be dead. He was named 'Nasty Nate' for obvious reasons since the poor puppy was filthy.

My son brought Nate to me. He was a young pup, about four to seven months old. He loved his 'grandma' (that is me by the way). For a very long time, he would not leave my side, and the sound of loud trucks terrified him.

Today this sweet boy, Nate, is living the good life now with me on six acres. I will never forget the first time I let him run around the yard. He had the biggest smile on his face while his ears were flopping in the wind as he ran freely. It was the best feeling to give that much happiness to a dog who so deserved to be treated well and loved.

Yes, I am a bit embarrassed to say this, but we are certainly friends by now, so I know you won't tell anyone this, right? I sing three songs to him each morning and end with "You Are My Sunshine." He rolls over and I rub his belly as he makes nice little Nate sounds. As I am writing this story, it is a very rainy day and Nate is still in bed sleeping away. He is older now and becoming a very quiet, loving, spoiled boy. But I am of the belief all animals should be spoiled.

I can't ever see my life without a pet. So, the next time I need one, you will go to the shelter and pick out one for me, right?

HERE, HOLD MY WINE MOMENT:
Adopt, don't shop! The best thing you can do in your life is to experience the unconditional love an animal can bring to you.

Chapter 38: Robin's Fresh Kill for Dinner

Time to take shot of something strong here!

∼

I MET A REALLY NICE COUPLE AT AN APPLE CIDERY ONE DAY, AND we became fast friends. They would come to my house for dinner sometimes, and I would go to their house, too. One night, they were supposed to come to my home and be there about 6:00 pm. About 5:30 pm, I opened my gate so they could get in my yard, and at 5:35 pm, someone was ringing my doorbell.

So, I went to the door, thinking the couple came early. Instead, it was two hunters in full-on camouflage apologizing to me stating they had been hunting in the farm down from me. They shot a doe (a female deer – how many of you are singing that song now?) and asked if it was OK to retrieve her from my property. I told them, "Of course, but I have people coming for dinner in a few minutes, so is there a way you can get her out of here before they come? I don't want them to think dinner was THAT fresh." They laughed and said they would get her out of there as quickly as possible.

When the doorbell rang the next time, it was my friends, who showed up about ten minutes early. They explained to me that the hunters were loading the gutted deer into the back of their Mazda sedan. I laughed and said, "Obviously, they are city hunters."

We all got a pretty good laugh out of that story.

$\mathcal{H}$ERE, HOLD MY WINE MOMENT:
I really do have some strange things that happen to me, now don't I? Want to come over for dinner and see what fun things we can come up with that I can write about?

Chapter 39 - The Final Chapter - Love - Are You Hiding Out There, Or Just Aging Like a Fine Wine?

Love can be like fine wine. Sometimes you need to age the wine before it is at its peak. But, if you let some wine go too long, you will spoil the wine. Don't turn into vinegar!

Well, you finally got to the end. Thank you for hanging in there with me to figure out what was the one thing missing from my life. Unless you peeked first, which I know the ones who actually did that – BUSTED!!!

As you have read, I have been through a lot of experiences, but trying to find love has eluded me.

I've had those who have made me 'think' I was important, but they did not really make me important enough. I've had those who had others in their life: some a wife, some an ex-wife, some a girlfriend and/or fiancé, and some even had the ex-girlfriend who took precedence over me.

Now before you get upset with me, I have made mistakes, but I do not sell myself short. Yes, I've been tempted by those who say they want me, but when called to the table to be the only one before I would go further, they will not leave for varied reasons.

So, until the right guy who can appreciate a really good woman and who wants a real relationship finally enters my life, I will continue to work, do things with my friends, and continue to be happy with life.

ERE, HOLD MY WINE MOMENT:
You do realize when I do finally find my special someone, I will write about the experience and let you know. But to find the one who finally will forsake all others to really want to be with me, then and only then will I be able to say to them…"Here, Hold My Wine!"

Some of Robin's Favorite Vineyards and Wines

I started off tasting sweet wines like a lot of new tasters do. I have since graduated with my palette. I have to admit, there are not many wines I do not like because they are so many different situations and meals that the right wine can fit in perfectly.

~~

Cooper Vineyard – Now named 53rd Winery & Vineyard
13372 Shannon Hill Rd, Louisa, VA 23093

Norton

A grape which was first cultivated in Virginia, and is now the official grape of the State of Missouri.

Sweet Rhapsody

Fantastic white table wine, known by myself and a good wine friend as 'Talk about your neighbors' wine. Great wine for sitting around on a hot summer's day and eating lite fare of cheese and crackers for fantastic conversations.

Sweet Louisa – 'Welch's Grape Juice on steroids'

Although my palette has changed, this is still a great starter wine.

Noche

First Chocolate wine in Virginia – Received a gold medal. A fantastic dessert wine especially when served in a chocolate cup. Guests love this wine.

~

Pollak Vineyard
230 Newtown Rd, Greenwood, VA 22943

Cabernet Sauvignon Reserve 2009

Honestly, I love everything I taste at this winery. The winemaker is unbelievable. I actually take buying parties to this winery. Fantastic staff and the wines are fantastic.

~

Upper Shirley Plantation Vineyard
600 Shirley Plantation Rd, Charles City, VA 23030

Sparkling

This winery really has a beautiful location on the James River. They have really great white wines and their reds are unbelievable. They have the best restaurant so be sure to make a reservation. You will not be disappointed!

～

Vidon Vineyard
17425 NE Hillside Dr, NE
Newberg, Oregon

Pinot Noir

Hans Clone Pommard – any year is great. This is one I am going to make it to one day. For now, I order a case every year to keep a supply on hand.

～

Domaine Chandon Winery
1 California Dr, Yountville, CA 94599
Napa Valley, California

Red Sparkling

Outstanding – you can only get this wine from the vineyard. I order a case every year.

～

Del Dotto Estate Winery & Caves
1055 Atlas Peak Road
Napa, CA 94558

Unique wine tasting in the caves.

Cabernet Sauvignon 2011

This bottle's grapes were grown on Howell Mountain.

Russian River Valley Zinfandel 2013

Letting this one 'cook' a bit longer, but cannot wait to try
- Tasted from the barrel in 2014 and was bottled for me.

~

Abbadia Ardenga il Poggio
Via Romana, 139, 53024 Torrenieri SI
Montalcino, Italy

Brunello 2004

Drank this one and it was fantastic. Still makes wines the
old way. Winemaker/owner gave us a special tasting in 2010.
Beautiful location.

~

Chateau Morrissette Winery
291 Winery Rd SW, Floyd, VA 24091

Old Dog Blue

It's a great standby wine that Virginians can get from a
grocery store to share!

References

Chapter 2 - Brad Lachman Productions in association with Operation Prime Time and Paramount Domestic Television, *Solid Gold, 1980-1988.*

Chapter 9 - Harry N. Ambrams, The Joys of Wine (New York, 1975), page 154.

Chapter 11 - "I Heard It Through the Grapevine" ©Copyright 1966 by Motown Records, written by Norman Whitfield and Barrett Strong. All Rights Reserved.

"Smile" ©Copyright 1954 by Bourne Co. Copyright Renewed All Rights Reserved.

Section 3 - Bowie, David. "Changes, Live." *YouTube* - https://youtube.com/watch?v=xMQoRyyo1yE.

Chapter 37 - "You Are My Sunshine" ©Copyright 1939, written by Jimmie Davis and Charles Mitchell.